flow

Beth Kephart

flow

The Life and Times of Philadelphia's Schuylkill River

Temple University Press
Philadelphia

TEMPLE UNIVERSITY PRESS
Philadelphia, Pennsylvania 19122
www.temple.edu/tempress

Design by Phillip Unetic, uneticdesign.com

Excerpt from "Leaving the Temple in Nîmes" from *Above the River:
The Complete Poems*, by James Wright, introduction by Donald Hall.
Copyright © 1990 by Anne Wright. Reprinted by permission of Farrar,
Straus and Giroux, LLC.

Frontispeice: George Cooke, *View on the River Schuylkill,* 1812. Print and
Picture Collection, The Free Library of Philadelphia.

Library of Congress Cataloging-in-Publication Data

Kephart, Beth.
Flow : the life and times of Philadelphia's Schuylkill River / Beth Kephart.
    p. cm.
  Includes bibliographical references.
  ISBN-13: 978-1-59213-636-0 (hardcover : alk. paper)
  ISBN-10: 1-59213-636-2 (hardcover : alk. paper)
   1. Schuylkill River (Pa.)—History.   2. Schuylkill River (Pa.)
—Description and travel.   3. Schuylkill River Region (Pa.)—Social life
and customs.   4. Schuylkill River Region (Pa.)—Economic conditions.
5. Philadelphia (Pa.)—History.   I. Title.
  F157.S33K47 2007   2006033201
  974.8'1—dc22

ISBN 978-1-59213-637-7 (paperback : alk. paper)

Printed in the United States of America

9 8 7

for Grandmom and Uncle Danny
in loving memory

and for those who dare to believe
in the beating heart of a river

CONTENTS

It was the color of the sky, and it ran clean. It was the color of shad and of the trees—sycamores, willows, oaks—that clustered near. It bent the reflection of the moon, then held it still. A man looked in, a woman did, and, startled, found themselves.

The Schuylkill River at its start is stone-coal country; there are hills in most directions. Blue Mountain. Second Mountain. Locust Mountain. Sharp Mountain. In Tuscarora there are covert springs, and this is where the east branch of the river begins—a trickle, not even a stream. It will wend its way between hills and across valleys before it joins with the west branch near Schuylkill Haven. It will course many miles more and take a turn through Philadelphia before it yields to the Delaware River, which will empty into a long-nosed bay before yielding to the sea.

The river is cumulative. It harbors the floating oddments of towns like Auburn, Reading, Birdsboro, and Valley Forge. It widens and rises at the intersection of creeks that turn toward it. There is dust in its waters, the churn of bones. There are the remains of islands and animals, perch and catfish, broken branches and water-logged seeds. You might find the cross-frame of a kite in its silt, or the last page of a diary, or the buckles of a soldier's shoe, or the chunky afterthought of anthracite. You might find the flint tip of a spear. That's the thing about this river: You have to imagine it to see.

William Penn took a canoe up the Schuylkill during his second trip to Pennsylvania—a pale man with a square face cutting the current with a paddle, his eyes on a rabble of low-flying pigeons, or on a beaver's well-built dam, or on the smoke rising from a Lenni Lenape fire. There would have been no sound of machines, no insistent hum of industry, but corn was being torn from its husk, no doubt, and a mother was calling for her child. Penn heard whatever a man could hear, afloat on that river, in a boat carved from a tree.

One might have hoped for a more spellable name, or for something more suggestive of a poem. But *Schuylkill*, once spelled *Skokihl*, means nothing more than Hidden Creek, and it was a Dutch navigator, Arendt Corssen, who did the christening. This was the middle of the seventeenth century, and it was bulrush season. The place where the Schuylkill meets the Delaware River was obscured and inauspicious the day that Corssen happened on it. In the spring, shad had to fly, not swim, to get upstream: The water at this junction was that shallow. Hidden Creek, Corssen thought to himself, and that's how the river got its name.

The Lenni Lenapes had better names for their river: *Ganshowahanna,* they called it, which means "falling waters." *Manayunk,* they also called it, which translates into "where we drink." The Indian names suggest a sound and a taste, but Schuylkill River is a navigator's label, a name for those who are headed somewhere. Be on the lookout, the name suggests. Turn your craft this way.

The river, all those years ago, took you somewhere. It took you (if you were entering it from its southern tip, if you were in a canoe, or on a boat, or on a makeshift raft) north and also west. You were moving against its current, but you were following its line. You were Dutch or you were Swedish or you were a Quaker exile from England, and you went the way the river went, between its crags, against its falls, through its shoals of determined shad, above its beds of mussels.

As a young man, Benjamin Franklin wandered beside the river beneath the big trees on its east shore. He'd come up from town, through fields of swine and cattle, past fruit trees and the bark of wild turkeys. He'd meet his friends by the banks, or else walk or sit alone. In winter, the trees would be barren; river ice would crunch up against the shore. In summer, it would be cool beneath the oak trees and thick with the smell of wildflowers and herbs, the drone of bees and flies. At the river's intersection with Spruce Street, where Franklin would meander, Pastor Morgan Edwards and his parishioners could be found getting ready for a dunk in the holy Schuylkill waters.

Bears once prowled near the banks of the Schuylkill, as did the occasional panther. Wolves were feared and greedy, and there were snakes, minks, hazel hens, cranes, woodchucks, squirrels, foxes, rabbits, not so many deer as one might think, and beavers that fishermen somehow trained to hunt and retrieve for them.

America's most active botanists lived and worked beside the Schuylkill. The gardens planted there were written of in postcards, in books, in letters travelers sent back home. There was John Bartram and his studies and his seed house, his sprouting things. There was William Hamilton and his Woodlands, Lemon Hill and Gray's Ferry. There was Meriwether Lewis coming partway across the country to be mentored in the art of flora hunting by the ambitious Benjamin Smith Barton. There was the river, always, and what grew there, and its wayward springs.

War would come to the Schuylkill, and so, of course, would fever. Ships heavy with anthracite, cattle, timber, and more would jam in both directions; wharves would overtake the banks; fishermen would complain. By the turn of the nineteenth century, the river was being diverted to local homes through bored spruce and yellow pine logs and the clever machinations of the Water Works. A few years later it was being dammed with hickory logs to satisfy the city's emphatic thirst.

It was only a matter of time before the Schuylkill below the dam became a liquid trash heap—something to cross, not something to see. Detritus would be wheeled to the river's bank and dumped— a steaming mess. Slaughterhouse remains would be dumped as well, not to mention whale oil, dead people, old furniture, broken plates, hair ribbons, clipped fingernails, the bones from a previous night's fowl, the pages of a book no one could finish. The river had turned the color of mud, the color of the noise on city streets.

But a river stands for something even after the silence is gone. Even after the wolves and the panthers and the hazel hens are gone, there are other stories, big as myths. A river still begins at covert springs, and it still flows out to sea. It still floats the moon on its back at night, still stares out at the faces staring in, still dreams.

flow

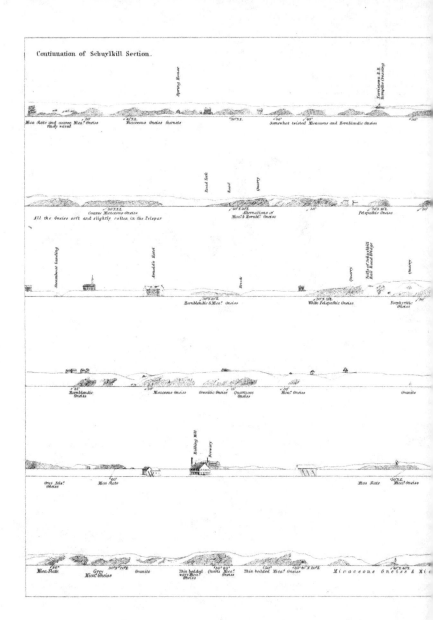

14

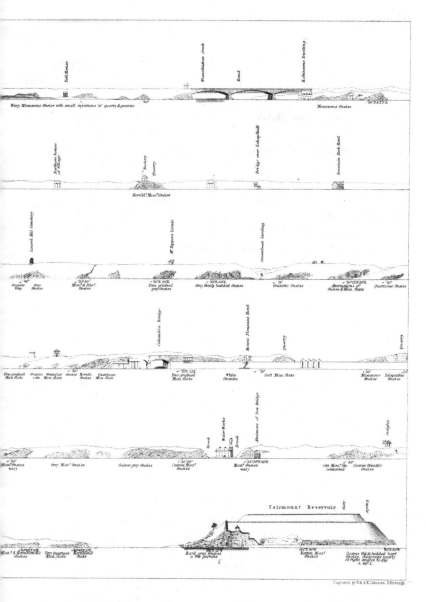

Pennsylvania Geological Survey, final section cut, including Lemon Hill and Fairmount Reservoir, 1858. Philadelphia Water Department Historical Collection.

Rising

From within the fissure I rise, old as anything.

The gravel beneath me slides. Blueback herring and eel, alewife and shad muscle in to my wide blue heart, and through. The smudged face of a wolf pools on my surface, and for that one instant I go blind.

Hemlock to either side. Nut trees. Laurel copses. The stony backs of snapping turtles on the shore, muskrat, shrew, and from the unlanterned forest, the bark of a fox, the *skith skith skith* of snakes over leaves, the prowl of a bobcat, and when it rains the rain is its own kind of song, not just a drumming, but a lyric.

Were there language, I'd be my own lone letter.

Like all rivers the Schuylkill is the product of crustal deformations and time. It begins unspectacularly, in the Appalachian Mountains of Schuylkill County. It winds, widens, speeds, and slows along a southeastern course, over Precambrian and Paleozoic rocks, over shale and clay, until it finds its way to the Delaware River, draining some 1,916 square miles in the process, and doing this day after day.

Bear

He breathes clouds in and breathes them out. There has been the long sleep of winter, and now as he stands near to my edge—bits of sticks in his matted fur, a lightning strike of white across his chest— he is besieged by smells. The curls inside leaves. The green cracking the earth. The beginnings of berries. If he has spent the winter dreaming wings—moths and birds and hoppers—he is hungry now for fish.

The moon is high, it is afloat—yellow and generous as fruit. A breeze blows in from a place beyond the bend, and I begin to break apart.

On the rise of the hill there is a she-bear waiting.

For bears, for wolves, for panthers, for muskrats, minks, and deer, for huge wild turkeys, for flocks of pigeons, for frogs and hoppers, for most anything one might imagine, the river was a haven.

Ganshowahanna

The sky is theirs: The hunters after the bear, the Thunderers and Horned Serpent of last night's storm, and the souls on the long, white trail—rising.

It was just yesterday that the Lenni Lenape boy and his father stood at my shore shadding with the claw of a bird and a net of knitted hemp. A bead had worked itself loose from the boy's black wampum—a kernel of grief sunk down and in among bones and stones, surrendered seeds, the bulrushes that once released themselves from the earth and drowned.

Today, in the smoky aftermath of the storm, in the mood of mourning, I ride the humped back of that dark whelk. It is the eleventh day of a mother's dying, and soon the skies will change again. Her heart soul will ascend to the heavens, on its Sky Journey. Her blood soul will hover ever close.

The Unami tribe of the Lenni Lenapes was the first known group of humans to settle along the Schuylkill, a river they called Ganshowahanna. Theirs was a spirit world rooted in a deep respect for nature. The stars overhead told stories of bear hunts and weather, eternity. The dead were said to have two souls—the soul of the heart and the soul of the blood. On the twelfth day of mourning, the heart soul ascended to the heavens. The blood soul, for its part, remained earthbound, a sometimes haunting, sometimes companionable ghost.

Howling

I thought it was an owl in the middle of the night, but it was the boy they had sent out among the wild grapevines and twining trees to find his own Manito—the boy in breech-clout and moccasins, a feather quilt upon one shoulder. I had seen him go. I had heard his famished cries all through the night and then the day and then the next night. Then there was a silence like a death, and then a waiting.

I was afraid for him.

I could not leave my banks and save him.

Darkness and day. Darkness and day. Clouds that bear the face of time, and a boy becomes a man.

Out into the woods, by the river, adolescent Indian boys were sent to fast and to come to terms with their own fears. It was in this way that they found their Manitos and became men.

Flight

Now he fells another tulip tree. Rims it in fire and axes it to the ground, then measures off a length and axes it again, burns the inside out, puts a stone adze to it, carries it to my edge, and sets it down. So that it trails the smell of smoke, this shallop. So that it is the sound of a blade in pulp as it rides my back this morning.

It is March, and the fog has lifted. The sturgeon are thick. The lamprey eels have latched themselves to the shad that have come up from the bay, turning my surface the color of purpose—of fish backs and of this floating, painted man whose spear points down from the sky.

Now the sturgeon take to the air and fly, and I find myself flying with them. I shatter and I bead—rain back down onto myself, less than I've been. This season's fish are bigger than any bird I've ever seen, bigger than the menace of a storm-soaked cloud. I feel their size all over me.

The shallop shudders with the thrashing of fish. The man with the spear shudders, too—rocks back and forth, tips this way, tips the other, until, just like that, he has fallen into me.

His hair swims away from him like so many black minnows.

It has been said that the Atlantic sturgeon once so crowded the Schuylkill River that one could walk across it on their backs during the spawning season. Armored with bony scutes, these anadromous fish with tubelike mouths are creatures from another time, throwbacks to the age of dinosaurs. In their eagerness to get upriver, the sturgeon were said to fly—hurtle through the air toward their destination.

Found

You know how the bulrushes grow: straight up and without fanfare, tufts of brown and a rattle of seeds at the tall stalk's stem. You know how they are hearth to fish and duck, to the birds that sing—how they cluster and, in the sweetest gesture of protection, fail to disclose.

But then a man, a stranger, his face a paler shade of flesh, his flag the color of fish eyes, his posture the posture of a man who should pass on by, finds himself out on that other river and, suddenly onto something, draws my veil of bulrushes aside. At the very place where I leak out of myself, where my long unspooling ends, where I am narrow, yes, and shallow, yes, he finds me, paddles through, and history's changed.

I have nothing to gain. I have nothing, right there, to offer. Did he expect more? Could he not see how far I'd come? I beach him, and he tries again. I beach him, and he breaks—turns his boat back amidst the circus act of shad. He yanks at the bulrushes, slaps at the buzz of the bugs, drags his hand across his forehead, and returns to wherever he's come from—the turtles yelling obscenities, though he's too full of schemes to hear.

As if I needed another name, he calls me Hidden Creek. As if I needed further examination, he spreads the word.

A grotesque failure of the imagination.

History has it that the first European to voyage up the Schuylkill was a man named Arendt Corssen of the Dutch East Indies Company. The river itself wasn't easy to find, for the bulrushes were in bloom and masked the narrow opening where the Schuylkill finally empties into the Delaware River. Probably in honor of the river's clever disguise, this new waterway was called the *Skokihl*, which means Hidden Creek.

Swarm

He was shalloping upstream. The sky was nothing special. He was oar in, oar out, oar in, and mostly he leaned east, the pit of a peach rolling about by his feet in his hollowed-out canoe. Not a pretty sound, never is.

It had been a season of fat turkeys and pompous pheasants. The swans were absurdly full of themselves. Had you asked me, I would have called for an interregnum of birds, but then the flock of wild pigeons swarmed—came calamitously upon us. One wing woven of countless wings. One beak. One feather. One swarm. Thick, dark, ominous, near as an overlord, a storm.

And there was no sun.

And the noise was no less exquisite than a roar.

And that's when William Penn laid down his oar and stood imperfectly upright in the shallop. As if it were his Quaker fate to touch the underbelly of a many-birded bird.

In the incomparable *Watson's Annals of Philadelphia and Pennsylvania*, published in 1857, rumors mix with reportage, incidents with opinions. William Penn, the city's fair-minded Quaker founder, is engagingly described and so, for that matter, are peaches. And then there's this bit of fabulous hearsay: "Wild pigeons . . . were like clouds, and often flew so low as to be knocked down with sticks."

Temptation

What you have not considered is this: My senses are not yours.
My eyes are also my thousand water ears. I do not touch; I feel.

So that when the smoke rises in the distance I can tell whether it comes
from Indian or kiln. When a song is sung, I know its source. I know
the weather before you do, and I have nothing to fear when a panther
stands near on a rock above my surface. My face is not what floats.

All of which is a preliminary to saying: I knew the white-faced
crowds would come. I knew they'd find their way from the other bank
of the other river—through swamp, through creek, past the curious
gaze of the Lenni Lenapes, past vines and whortleberries, chasing
wild turkey, chasing quail, running fast from the fevers they like to
claim are distilled beneath the understory of the ancient trees.

I was another country then. I was temptation. And what precisely lay
to my west? What lay beyond my falls?

There is a white boy borrowing a painted man's shallop. There is a
girl with yellow hair and a high-collared dress stepping in beside the
boy, her braids gone loose with weather.

She slips her hand inside my skin, leaves a small effervescence in
her wake.

While the Lenni Lenapes had traveled east over miles and miles of uncharted land to find
the region that would become Philadelphia, European settlers had traveled west, by boat.
Despite William Penn's meticulous plan for the city—a plan that called for the equal distri-
bution of settlers between the area's two circumscribing rivers—most congregated as close
as possible to their first point of entry, along the Delaware River. They lived in caves and
mud houses before they began to build with bricks. They turned patches of forest into open
air with almost frightening efficiency. Still, they wondered what lay beyond the thicket of
forest, the rumors of beast and fowl.

Ice Storm

You want to blame me for how we together broke apart, abandoned the little rules we each had lived by. You want me implicated in the fracture of time, in my viscous letting loose, my rising. Something you had made was broken. Something you had thought to be true was rendered false. Some line you supposed had been laid down between us was vanquished—leaving chunks of ferryboats among my chunks of ice, chunks of ruptured trees, a catastrophic bruising.

That moan you heard was my soul in repeated shatters. That cleaving apart was my remorse. You have your list of lost things; I have mine. How I abandoned myself. How I could not fight to save me.

Among the many extraordinary weather events recorded in *Watson's Annals* is the flood of February 1733, during which, it is written, "the ice in Schuylkill broke up with a fresh and came down in cakes of great thickness, in a terrible manner, breaking great trees where the flood came near the low land." The flood was considered epic.

Catfish

Funny how a man will boast over a river's plenitude.

"In former times it was quite different. Old Godfrey Shrunk, when about 74 years of age, a well known fisherman near the Falls in his younger days, has told me he could often catch with his dip-net 3000 catfish in one night ! Often he has sold them at two shillings a hundred. The perch and rockfish were numerous and large; often he has caught 30 to 80 lbs. of a morning with a hook and line." Excerpted from *Watson's Annals;* the old man's name was actually "Schronk."

Comet

There is a hill that rises near the Falls, on the east side. They call it Faire Mount, and when a wolf stands on its crest, the ground below him trembles; when the wind tries to blow straight through, it is separated from itself; and if I am envious of anything, it is of those who might ascend and watch as the stars settle in upon my scrim. To see myself from above myself, in the iris black of night.

Several sunsets ago there was a girl alone on the mount, perhaps a young woman. A thick, brown to-the-ground coat and a hat on her head, a woolen scarf at her neck; no, she was just on the cusp of being a young woman. But she was there and alone and the sun was falling and it was that one untraveled instant before the gloaming. Simply put, the girl was not lonesome. She was keen with something close to privilege. She was unafraid in a world still full of wolves.

Time and wind. The bone chill of January. The alert way she sat on the mount, with the night sliding forward and the sky antique, and suddenly (though it must have been there before) a comet. Ice for its head. Dust and ions in the seeming whoosh of its aftermath. The smell of methane and ammonia and burn, and looking up to it, I was looking up through it, its second self already needled on my surface.

What she must have seen. What she must have guessed of my own great wanting in that high howl of winter.

Comets have entered the theater of the Philadelphia skies at inconstant intervals since time immemorial. Among the first recorded by our forefathers was the one that appeared on January 22, 1742.

Confidante, Three Days Afterwards

Cold outside, and dark. I hear her coming. The meadow and marsh between her house and myself must be slick with risen ice, and if the wild swine have any optimism, then wild swine will be about, but she is running. She has pulled on her woolen coat and taken up a candle in a glass. She is running her way from chimneyed houses, past market stalls and taverns, toward the trees and the paths between the trees, between stretches of gooseberries and bilberries and wild plums and grapes, the fruit only a thought, for it is winter.

She knows her way to me.

And knows I listen.

John Bartram

He has the patience of seeds and a genius for walking, a long way of standing at the bend near my end where he has made his garden, where he stores and sorts, where he reads the books he borrows and puts a name on things. Knows the hierarchy of God to man and never reverses the order. Seeks shade. Rejoices in sweet gum and black willow, river birch and alder. Holds a disk of glass to one eye and a small found something in his hand, always a found something in his hand. Uses the word *preserve*. Submits to sunsets.

Yesterday he sank his two bare feet into my tide, cupped out a baby turtle that had gotten misdirected by an eddy, and called for William, his son. They passed the turtle hand to hand, then, admiring its shell, its anxious feet, its timid head—turning it over, slow, so that William might draw it later, so that John might write it into one of his letters to Peter Collinson.

Afterwards John leaned in close and returned the turtle to where it had come from. Forfeiting possession for the sake of a species.

Born in 1699 on a farm in Darby Township, the self-educated and self-effacing John Bartram would spend his life in pursuit of seeds and roots, traveling along the entire eastern corridor and as far west as the Ohio River in search of specimens that he might cultivate in his own garden, which was located at an ideally high point near the river, or send off in sleeves to friends. Of Bartram's nine children, it was his son William who carried forth the Bartram legacy, ultimately becoming a recognized expert in the flora and fauna of the south and publishing, in 1791, *Travels through North and South Carolina, Georgia, East and West Florida, Cherokee Country, etc.*, a journal of his botanic explorations. Among the many visitors to the Bartram home were Thomas Jefferson, Benjamin Franklin, James Logan, David Rittenhouse, and George Washington. *Franklinia alatamaha*, a fragrant tree with sweet white flowers originally discovered along a Georgia river and later propagated in the Bartrams' Philadelphia garden, was named by William Bartram in honor of his father's friend.

Augustus Köllner, *Schuylkill River below Philadelphia,* 1841. Print and Picture Collection, The Free Library of Philadelphia.

Baptismal Rites

She ties her bonnet to the limb of a tree and sits on a rock to remove her satin slippers, but then she has the problem of her silk petticoat, which is dark green with a fringe of blue, and of her hidden hoops, and then of her hair, which falls in tight curls to her chin and is covered by a hood, and these things she wants to keep just as they are. She does not, in other words, wish to go farther. She stands with great unhappiness on my edge.

The others are not like her; they are eager. They are certain, moreover, of my own complicity in their forgiveness. Because of that, they confuse my current for God's hand upon their backs. I am the slight taste of fish, but to them, that's holy. I seep in through cloth and skin, and that's their proof of sure redemption.

But the woman has an apparent talent for self-determination. She watches the others and cannot transfer their conviction to herself. Cannot fall within the spell of Pastor Morgan Edwards, whose lively exhortations incite *Yes, Lords* from the others.

She takes a clump of wildflowers in her hand. She removes her bonnet from the limb of the tree, where she has tied it. She turns on her heel and leaves—goes back up the hill, to Spruce Street.

They will not make her fear, even now. They will not cage her in their religion.

"On the bank of the Schuylkill, at the end of Spruce street, there was, in the early times of the city, an oak grove, selected by the Baptist Society as a Baptisterion, to lead their initiates into the river to be baptized, as did John in Enon.

"Morgan Edwards, their pastor, who describes it as he saw it before the year 1770, (he arrived here in 1758) says of it—'Around said spot are large oaks affording fine shade—under foot is a green, variegated with wild flowers and aromatic herbs, and a tasteful house is near for dressing and undressing the Proseuches.' In the midst of the spot was a large stone, upon the dry ground, and elevated above it about three feet—made level on the top by art, with hewn steps to ascend it. Around this rock the candidates knelt to pray, and upon it the preacher stood to preach to the people." Excerpted from *Watson's Annals*.

State in Schuylkill

Sizzle is the smell of shad and pig over fire that bursts into smoke
and floats like a cloud right here, too close. The men are laughing.
Something about red-string Madeira and William Warner's punch,
the key that after so much winter would not convince the lock.
Someone telling the story of a whiskey run and another of a seine
that came up so fat with shad that it dropped a man straight to his
knees, tore a hole through the britches his missus was in no mood to
mend.

Next week the shad will rise again. Come upriver and blush me pink
with their useless enthusiasm. Run themselves into a wall of net, flip
tail to their death in these rich men's kitchen. Only the eyes that
never shut will be tossed back home, to me. Only the woman, in the
kitchen cooking, will engage her sympathy.

Founded in 1732, The Colony in Schuylkill (later renamed The Schuylkill Fishing Company of
the State in Schuylkill) was one of the oldest organizations of its kind—a men's social club
dedicated to hunting and fishing with more than a whiff of aristocracy about it. Their meeting
place was an elaborate facility with an ample kitchen, built on the west bank of the Schuylkill
on a one-acre parcel of William Warner's land, where the shad streamed by in almost over-
whelming abundance. Anyone who was anybody was invited to the fishy feasts right up
through 1822, when the new dam at Fairmount Park impeded the shad. Determined to keep its
elite traditions intact, State in Schuylkill floated the club buildings four miles downstream to
Rambo's Rock, across from Bartram's Garden, where the fish still congregated.

Skating Party

James Mason is the bravest. He'll test my strength. Walk out in his sly
shoes, his arms out, his blades slung over one shoulder. Jaunty count-
ing for something, and his face raw to the wind.

He'll slide, and I'll hold. He'll carry on, west, and the boys on the east
bank will begin their hollering back at him, "The ice won't hold," but
he'll say, "I'm going forward." Announce it, then announce it loud,
without turning, for it takes something to keep your jaunty up, and
only I ever know for certain how solid as stone and slick I am. How
wide he might go, how far he might fall, how thorough I am with the
cold. There will be leaves trapped on my surface, colors of fall. There
will be twigs and the wings of a bug. An iced-in mitten and the torn-
out pages of a book and the leaking orange of a dulled-by-winter sun.
His jaunty full upon him now. His walk tripping into a run, and he'll
leap and land, his blades still on his shoulder, and I'll be solid. "Ice is
for taking," he'll turn this time and call, and the others will holler
again from the edge. Strap on their skates and razor in.

Imagine taking a needle to the point of blood on your palm. Imagine
drawing that needle around and around, leaning in on it, forcing an
edge, tearing at the creases and the lifelines, the ridges and slightest
hills that forecast your happiness. Imagine the skin giving way.

That's skating.

Philadelphians loved to skate, and given the watery conditions of the city—the two prime
rivers, the criss-cross of creeks, the profusion of ponds—there were plenty of opportunities
when the cold set in and the waterways turned to ice. Of course there were risks involved
and many a rescue required when patches of thin ice gave way beneath the skaters' feet.

Tipsy

Warm nights are bliss. When the owls hover near and the crickets are chorus, when the moon shows some part of itself. The stars are legends. The smell is smoke from chimneystacks and the steam off fresh manure, the flame about a wick, dogwoods zealously blooming. Warm nights, most nights, are a quieting, a sanctified less. I flow south, I tumble south, and yet some part of me is still.

Last night was different. I couldn't hear the crickets for all the hooting of young men. I couldn't smell, because what is sweet cannot be sensed outside of quiet. I couldn't rest for the spill of young men, hurrying back home, by means of ferry, from the tavern.

It was the red-headed one with the streak of copper freckles, that most notorious James Mason, who launched what became their ferry game. He who, standing too close to the ferry's edge, began to lean, allowing the uncorked bottle in his hand to lean, allowing his red wine to dribble in. "Let's get her drunk," he said, meaning me, but speaking to the others, each of whom was willing to let his wine run free over the gunwale.

I'd never been so blood-colored. I'd never felt so clobbered, come morning.

Crossings

There was never anything that I could do: I am this wide. I am this deep. A tad voluptuous, but only in places. So that someone on the west would stand calling to someone on the east, on occasion, or a man in a canoe would offer passage to a friend, or a ferry would set passengers afloat at a mostly unforgivable price, if you consider the actual distance.

It was Washington who perceived in me the possibility of an ally. Who recognized that the British were coming and that his men would need an expedient escape—a something solid at their feet, an accommodation for boots, for arms, for orders. He was the one who called for a floating bridge—part logs, part scows—which in due time, and with some difficulty, was built. Hardly wide enough for a horse and his man, hardly secure, end to end, but the bridge held, at least for then, and one after the other they did come, ragged and a little scared. The sound of the beating war upon me. A boy in the rear going by foot, with a drum.

Afterwards, when they were gone, when there was the distant smell of gunsmoke, the sound of dying, I imagined the days Washington likely spent imagining me, drawing a finger down a map of my curves.

Until the High Street Bridge (at present-day Market Street) was opened in 1805, those who lived in, did business with, or came upon the city had to contend with the challenge of getting from one bank to the other. Though vulnerable to floods and notoriously dangerous, pontoons—floating barges that had been lashed together and secured to both banks of the river—provided one solution. George Washington instructed General Israel Putnam to supervise the construction of a bridge floated on scows to support the Continental Army on its way to Brandywine. Later that bridge was cut down, its pieces tucked away in river marshes, so that the British, whose ambition of occupying Philadelphia was, for a while, realized, could not make use of it.

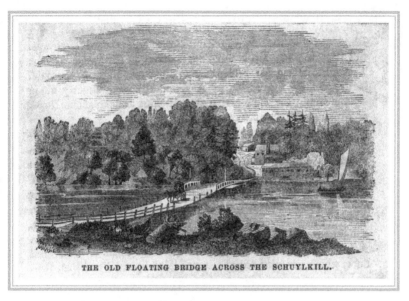

THE OLD FLOATING BRIDGE ACROSS THE SCHUYLKILL.

The Old Floating Bridge across the Schuylkill. Print and Picture Collection,
The Free Library of Philadelphia.

Fort Mifflin

There is no flowing past it to the sea. There are no distractions. All day and all night long, the brandished muskets of the British, the leaden suns of cannon balls, the sounds men make when they are dying. The skies will catch on fire, then go black. The smoky trousers of ghosts will pass overhead, and there is the chinking and chinking of bullets against the shattered shells, the broken glass, the hardened muck of my bottom.

He is lying flat on his back in the mud and seeing every star that hangs above me as a hole in the sky, a piercing. His lungs are smoke. His arms are emptied out and hollow. It is November, and soon everything will go entirely to ice, freeze the enemy ships into their places. Soon General George Washington and his troops will dig in at Valley Forge, and soon all the Loyalists and their wives and their prostitutes and the general who invaded Philadelphia will dance where they don't belong and eat what isn't theirs. And now the stars in the sky are the rebels who have died, the ones who won't be coming home to girls they'd promised to make wives.

From the island across the way, from the *Vigilant,* the *Roebuck,* the *Somerset,* the *Isis,* the British are mounting their last offensive, fixated now on obliterating Mud Island, which has stood so vehemently in their way. "We're breaking their supply lines, men," the colonel says. "We're giving General Washington time."

But already his pockets are bloodied with the talismans of lost men, with the buttons from their uniforms, with letters written home. Already his lungs are vapors. Already he cannot say what he will be obliged to say to the mothers and fiancées and wives and children who don't know for certain what he will be obliged to tell them, over and over again.

With the defeat of Washington's army at Brandywine and the subsequent occupation of Philadelphia by British and German troops, British General George Howe seemed precariously close to consolidating his victories and winning the war against the colonies. But before he could battle the revolutionary soldiers who had fanned out around Philadelphia, Howe had to gain access to some 240 British supply ships anchored in Delaware Bay. Some 200 courageous soldiers made it their business to thwart Howe's plans, attacking the British ships from their stronghold on Mud Island, near the juncture of the Delaware and Schuylkill rivers. Though the rebels ultimately lost the battle in mid-November 1777, they'd gone a long way toward winning the war—giving Washington sufficient time to dig in at Valley Forge before Howe could free his supplies.

Independence

This is the way a raptor flies: north to south from August through December, south to north in the months of April and May. Coasting on deflected winds when she can, cresting on the lift of thermals, hunting down voles and mice and toads, sometimes finishing her meal in the sky.

It was one of those effulgent days. Everything seemed touched by the intimation of precious metal—platinum on the limbs of trees, silver in the tips of flowers, gold glinting. It was also silent—an absolute and lovely silence, no one about, no gunfire in the distance, the sturgeon gone off to their spawning, the beavers finished with their dams. That's when I heard the she-hawk call. That's when I yearned— do you know the shape of yearning?—to lift up and up, to fly.

Wind rush and weather. Eyes that acutely see. A body attuned to the physics of lift and weight, thrust and drag.

For once give me the freedom of the skies.

On April 11, 1783, following eight years of fighting and inestimable losses, the Continental Congress declared an end to the Revolutionary War. Four years later, on September 17, 1787, the new Constitution of the United States was adopted, establishing legislative, executive, and judicial branches. George Washington, who had resigned his post as commander in chief of the American Revolutionary army two days before Christmas of 1783, was named the new country's first president.

Confession

Take it from me: There are no secrets. You think you've gone to the edge to cry alone, but I provide the testimony. You think you're talking to yourself, but yourself has me. You think your lover is the only one who knows of the kiss you stole on a midnight stroll along my shore from Spruce up to Walnut, and, my friend, you are deluded. I know which wildflowers you've come to pick. I know the fish that you've gone tender with, tossed back into my waters. I saw you steal that basket of eggs from beneath the tree that stands at the terminus of Locust Street.

I know what you said when the war was through.

What you wanted to confess to.

What you fear can't be forgiven.

Folly

They make their burdens mine. Animal fur and whiskey, powdered lime, split hemlock trees, a pair of extra walking boots, the wigwam that throws out the shade their spotted cow will stand in, the boy who comes with his father for the long, obstructed ride downstream, and none of it any good if they can't beat me at the Falls, if they can't make like they have wings.

Something in the way they shift. Something in the angle of their spines and the sound of their hollering, their hesitating and their sudden frantic speed, and I know it's coming—the dig in and the push out, the scramble at the rocks.

Many years, a drowning. A body dashed into my white spit. Bones sunk down with the calcium of catfish and of beaver, with turtle shells and the bright gold ring that marks the unmade promise.

Four miles north of Philadelphia, the Schuylkill crashed and foamed over the black reefs of the Falls—one of many geographic complications that made transporting goods up and down the river so difficult and dangerous. Hardy farmers nevertheless made a go of it, doing all that might be done to harness the river in their quest to send lumber, barrels, boxes, livestock, snuff, and so many other goods downstream. By 1794, according to J. Bennett Nolan, author of the indispensable *The Schuylkill,* Reading Boats were in service—sixty-foot-long constructions that could transport imposing quantities of goods. Their appearance each spring was, as he tells it, cause of both celebration and consternation.

Ice

I question their affection.

Toward the end of the eighteenth century, Philadelphians began to extract large chunks of ice from the Schuylkill—carve it straight out of the river in winter and haul it up to icehouses, where it remained until it was needed to chill food and water throughout the summer.

Air

They wanted everything. This new country as their own right home, the lands they'd come from or once longed for honored by leaves and buds and trees. So that the air went ripe with the smell of their experiments—with the hawthorn, hazel, and walnut trees sprung from the seeds Penn himself slipped into a ship; with the jambos and mimosas of Hamilton's hothouse; with the beginnings of a Chinese tallow tree, sent to Franklin by way of France.

Artichokes
Geraniums
Coral Trees
Azaleas
Birds of Paradise
Magnolias
Bananas
Camellias

And all of it foreign, all of it close and pungent, especially in July, when the sky will not rise and rarely falls.

Some of it stolen and transplanted for reasons only a river might imagine. Some of it the thing a child remembers, when in the height of fever.

Philadelphia quickly became the undisputed center of American botany—a hothouse of experimental farms and gardens. Seeds and cuttings would arrive in pockets, in letters, and between the pages of books. Seed shops became great venues of exchange. Robert Morris, a signer of the Declaration and a financier of the Revolutionary War, filled his greenhouses on the Schuylkill with natural oddities. William Hamilton was a prime Bartram customer— eager to prod a borrowed seed into life. The fields around Gray's Ferry became a garden lover's delight, and in yard after yard, gardens grew.

Laurel

He was imperfect and tall, and I loved him. I made myself still to hold his face. On that day the whole city had gathered on my either side and stood in an anticipatory hush until he, his horse, his entourage could be made out in the distance. And then the ladies straightening their hats, the men standing tall, and the boy in the white robe with the laurel wreath upon his head taking his ceremonial place beside the laurel arch. The gardens of Gray's Ferry were in bloom. The flags maintained their posture in the breeze. The lashed-together logs held west to east, and I quieted the fish, and I silenced the frogs, and I kept on keeping my waters right and calm.

I'm telling you: There was none greater. He was a man humbled by his own mistakes. A man for whom power was a vast responsibility, a most reluctant hero taking a people's crown.

For days afterward, I felt the tremble of his horse's hooves through the float of wood upon my surface.

The installation of George Washington as the country's first president involved a ceremonial horseback journey from Washington's home in Mount Vernon to the seat of the federal government in New York City. His crossing into Philadelphia over the Schuylkill at Gray's Ferry was, as reported by *Columbian Magazine*, entirely unforgettable: "About noon the illustrious Washington appeared, and as he passed under the first triumphal arch, the acclamations of an immense crowd of spectators rent the air, and the laurel crown, at that instant, descended on his venerable head.

"His Excellency was saluted on the common by a discharge from the artillery, and escorted into Philadelphia by a large body of troops, together with his excellency of the president of the state, and a numerous concourse of respectable citizens."

Soul

The difference between a man's soul and a cumulus cloud is that the cloud rubs out of its own accord and a man's soul never does.

Yesterday, Benjamin Franklin died after a year of suffering, and his soul has already risen, its color the color of sun through leaf. There's an eccentric quiver in the air, a strange disruption, and the idle talk along my banks is of him—the way he flirted with the possible and carried on for peace, how his wit was perpetually his wisdom.

Mid-April, and the trees are ripe, the birds returned. The clouds are slower in their passing.

The list of firsts attributed to Benjamin Franklin is famously diverse—first fire department, first subscription library, first police force—and then there's the lore about the kite he flew in the midst of an electrical storm. His death came on April 17, 1790, three years after he sat with fellow founders at the Constitutional Convention. Among the beloved things remembered in his will was the Schuylkill River, which he hoped would someday be made navigable with the funds he left behind.

Yellow Fever

It was a low-flying sheen that I could hardly see through.

It was a murderously persistent whine.

The eggs were slime.

I was too shallow.

Forgive me.

Drought overtook Philadelphia during the summer of 1793. As waterways began to run
dangerously low, flies and mosquitoes took awful advantage—turning every slick and stream
into breeding grounds. Meanwhile, in July, the first of what would become thousands of
refugees from Santo Domingo began appearing on the docks of the Delaware, seeking
political sanctuary while harboring, themselves, the strains of deadly yellow fever. The first
victims died soon after. Some 5,000 would die by November, taxing an ill-prepared medical
system and confounding physicians such as Benjamin Rush, who could not discern the cause
of the plague and whose best advice—to leave the city—was duly heeded by many.

Varnish

The only coat I wish to wear is Autumn's, before the leaves have loosened from the trees and when the mood is harvest.

George Cooke, *View on the River Schuylkill,* 1812. Print and Picture Collection,
The Free Library of Philadelphia.

The Hills

They walk up and back, shoulder to shoulder. Washington speaking. Morris shaking his wide, depleted face. Washington touching his hand to the ruined man's sleeve. Morris looking down and ashamed, and Washington wanting, I can feel how he is wanting, to find the one right thing to say in the midst of an incurable circumstance.

There is the indisputable scent of ripe azalea, the hunt of bees for pollen, a shadow cast by the old icehouse, but other than that: silence.

A buckle on one of Washington's shoes blazes intermittently with low-on-the-horizon sun.

As a wealthy merchant and member of the Continental Congress, Robert Morris played a crucial role in the American Revolution—using his private wealth to supply Washington's army with munitions and warm clothing and his influence to finance so many other aspects of the war. For close to thirty years, Morris maintained a sumptuous summer home on a cliff above the river's east bank. He called it The Hills, cherished its wildflowers and trees, created his own working farm and the nation's first icehouse, and planted pungent flowers in his famed greenhouse. Sunday dinner parties at The Hills were legendary, with guest lists including the likes of Washington, Franklin, and John Adams.

But by the end of the eighteenth century, ruined by soured speculative land deals and haunted by accusations that he had profited from the war, Morris found himself facing the probability of a long stint in a debtors' prison. Ashamed and diminished, he walked the banks of the Schuylkill with his friend George Washington in the days leading up to his arrest.

Unplugged

It's so dark and so foul-smelling, and they don't tell me where I am going, and didn't they think I'd miss the fish? Miss the slick backs of the turtles, the shade of the big trees, the float of leaves? I am afraid of teacups, I am a first-class claustrophobe, I am affronted by their spigots, and don't even speak to me of privies.

When they gush me on, when they yank me off, I am slivered into tears. I die of boredom in their buckets. Oh, the genius, Benjamin Latrobe. Channeling me out of myself through hollowed parts of trees. Pumping me into factories and sixty-three separate homes.

It is left to me to find my own salvation. To enter, at last, into the benediction of a young girl named Annie, who, tending a garden, chooses me. Pours me into a long-spouted can, carries me over her arm, and transports me out to the birds of paradise, the violet petals and sweet peas, the bath that has been drawn up for the swallows. Where I am let free. Where the sun is familiar and I transcend my usefulness.

A cat cozies up to the sweet peas and yawns. The child sits for a moment in the sun, dreaming herself to other places.

As citizens of the largest American city at the time, Philadelphians were beginning to worry about the future of their water supply. The well water that had long provided for the majority of homes and business establishments was growing tainted. River water wasn't as accessible as it increasingly needed to be. In 1798, Benjamin Henry Latrobe, an enterprising engineer, suggested channeling the Schuylkill to homes on the east side by means of bored pipes made of spruce and pine. Two pumping stations were built—one at Chestnut Street Wharf and one at Centre Square—and by the end of 1801, sixty-three homes, four breweries, and one sugar refinery were receiving their water through that system.

Meriwether Lewis

Lewis comes swaggering in from the west boasting of rifles, maps,
the trails he plans to blaze, time pressing. Announces what he's
mastered as a way of diminishing what he hasn't, and his eagerness is
brisk, efficient. Benjamin Smith Barton, Lewis's teacher in flora and
fauna, wants him to sit; Lewis walks ahead. Barton wants him to
think of similes—*smells like, tastes like, looks like*—and Lewis makes a
little fuss about all the learning he's come from before he attends to
Barton's long herbaceous story. Pistil, stamen, petal parts. The way
you snip this leaf from that stem, and how you press it. Labels to be
written on blotting paper in handwriting so upright it might actually
be read.

If only Barton himself were fit enough to take the trip; that's what
Barton's thinking. He'd give anything for the adventure, for the long
way west, along my sister rivers. Mud up to his knees, he supposes.
Birds in trees he's never seen, flowers that bloom big as the moon.
He's had enough of writing books and teaching. He wants to sleep
beneath the stars, enclose a seed in a letter home, name a bush after a
friend, and why not? Hasn't he earned it? Must he be so betrayed by
age—his own too many years, another man's too few?

Listen, I would say, if he would hear me.

Listen.

I myself am not all found out.

Before Thomas Jefferson's personal secretary, Captain Meriwether Lewis, could embark on
the cross-country odyssey that became known as the Lewis and Clark expedition, he needed
to fortify his knowledge of flora and fauna—learn to identify the new, trace a nut back to its
tree, operate a flower press, prepare plant labels. To advance Lewis's education, Benjamin
Smith Barton, a professor of botany at the University of Pennsylvania, accompanied Lewis
on exploratory trips along the Schuylkill.

Progress

The day before this day I heard a boy talking to his sister about dragons—their crenellated wings, their words of puff. He was professing his faith in their existence, while sitting on a rock, while watching his sister trace the fringe that is my edge with her longest, smartest finger. They had stopped fishing. It was near to noon. Their mother was high on the banks, making a chain of daisies beneath a lilac-colored parasol, talking to a man who did not seem to be their father.

I liked this boy; I liked his stories. I liked how his sister liked them, too. And though the minnows were deep in their afternoon clamor, I drew them upstream, north veering toward west, so that I might listen more closely to the boy's emphatic tale.

Air will taste like burn wherever a dragon has been. That's what the boy told his sister. Sky will look like a stain. Dragons run on big webbed feet and are the kingdom come.

It seemed to me that the boy was speaking of something that had happened long ago, been told to one who had told it to another who had passed it down to him. And I thought how comforting it must be to sit in the sun, in the mind of a legend. How comforting simply to tell a story that somebody sits to hear.

But the boy's dragon was no mere legend. It was, instead, a premonition, passed on, in code, to me.

The possibilities of the steam-powered engine captured the imaginations of self-taught inventors. In the summer of 1805, Oliver Evans, already contracted by the city of Philadelphia to build equipment capable of dredging the docks along the Schuylkill, heralded the coming of a steam-driven machine that could make its way across both water and land. Gathered along Market Street and up and down the river's banks, eager Philadelphians bore witness to the world's first Amphibious Dredge, a steam-powered vehicle that churned its way down Market Street before settling into the river and continuing its churning there.

Conflagration

That evening the sun had erupted low on the windowpanes at Howland's Tavern, and an old tabby with preternaturally brightened eyes had been out late, on the prowl, near my shore. And for no reason but for these that I've confessed to, I was alert to possibility, expecting the plummet of stars or the embittered moan of a tree. Such is the fate of an insomniac in winter: Even the smallest intensifying is a precursor of something. Every brightness within a darkness is a *frisson*.

Still, it was well past midnight when I saw the first lick of flames. When I realized that it wasn't moon but fire at Howland's—big ragged sheets of light and heat. Wind was blowing the fire east, and the bridge, the brand new bridge at High Street, lay in its path.

Whoever was the first among them was followed at once by others. There was the loud, urgent calling of voices, the hastened slamming of doors, the pounding of boots over the winter-hardened roads, the clanging together of buckets, jars, chamber pots, shovels—anything that was near to a door and good for grabbing. Some of them ran away from the tavern and some ran directly for it, but most of them headed straight for the bridge, as if their fierce wanting to save it would be enough to save it, as if they could talk a fire into a river. On the opposite shore a girl was crying.

It was the wind, in the end, that changed its mind. The wind that turned the fire about on its gaseous heel and sent it back west, where it might be tamed. I'd have been helpless, and that's the awful truth. I blistered for days, but no one noticed.

The cornerstone for the first elevated bridge across the Schuylkill was laid in 1800, and five years later construction of the 1,300-foot-long Permanent Bridge was complete. Just one year after that, on January 21, 1806, Howland's Tavern, located on the west bank, caught fire. For a frightening stretch of time, the bridge lay directly in the raging fire's path. In his popular history of West Philadelphia, Leon Rosenthal claims that five thousand Philadelphians rushed from their homes at 3 a.m., determined to save their connection to the eastern shore. The bridge was saved. Six years later it would be joined by the Upper Ferry Bridge at Spring Garden Street, a wooden-span bridge known to most as the Wernwag, after its designer.

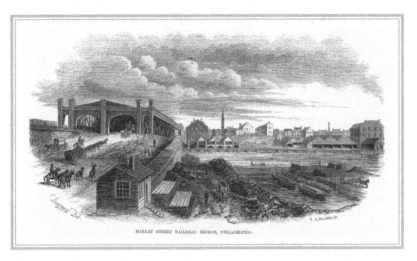

Market Street Railroad Bridge, 1805. Philadelphia Water Department Historical Collection.

Ornament

The perfectly preserved skull of a finch has worked itself loose from my clay belly and made its way to shore in the afternoon, a Sunday, when all but one of Breck's guests have gone off to sleep, extolling the bliss of seared venison and the powerful opinion of the whiskey. So that only one has come astride a borrowed mare that has sunk herself up to her knees in me.

When he dismounts it's like a cape being tossed off a pair of gallant shoulders. When the toes, the soles, the heels, the buckles of his boots splash in, I am turned back on myself. The man bends; I am sucked up into his coattails. He reaches; the skull of the finch is snatched from my shore. He turns the skull over in his palm before he stows it in his pocket. He begins to whistle some French tune. I conjure the pale woman with the long hair who will wear that skull upon her neck, when he returns to her.

Built in 1797 on the right bank of the Schuylkill, Sweetbrier was another country estate made famous by the hospitality of its owner, Sam Breck, who had come to Philadelphia by way of Boston in 1792 and would become known as the father of free schools. Breck's gardens cascaded down to the river. His horses pastured on the slopes. His guest lists tended to feature many French people, particularly those who had escaped the terror of the French Revolution.

Augustus Köllner, *Sweet Briar Mansion*, 1842.
Print and Picture Collection, The Free Library of Philadelphia.

Navigation

Oh, but I did wage war upon the men who dug me out and dammed me, who redirected all my flowing. I was a fist, a scourge, a seductress—pulling stones and sludge through their grinding gears, making sounds they couldn't account for, flooding them out where my veins were cut, introducing their best man to plague. I put the thought of bewitchery between the ears of their mules. I inculcated pirates. Whatever they pulled across me, I conspired to snap. Wherever they dug, I resisted. Whoever dared to think he had gotten somewhere was tossed straight off my back.

Did you think I would just lie here and take it? Did you think I couldn't anticipate the consequence of their insatiable need to tame me? *Eighteen dams. Twenty-three canals. One hundred and twenty locks, seventeen stone arch aqueducts, one tunnel ... thirty-one homes for toll and lock keepers.* And don't you think they might have seen it, too—the undoing of my beauty, my defacement, in exchange for hogs and combs and buttons, empty whiskey kegs?

For all of its watery possibilities, the Schuylkill River continued to present stiff obstacles to those who sought to use her as a means of transporting goods down from anthracite and farming country, of bringing lumber, oysters, melons, empty barrels, and new clothes upriver from ships that would harbor in the Delaware. For one thing, the river dropped more than 600 feet in elevation from its source in the mountains to the point where it emptied into the sea. For another, there was the growing inconvenience of the dams and nets that fishermen relied on to haul in a profitable catch.

After the chartering of the Schuylkill Navigation Company in 1813, work finally commenced on a series of dams and canals—an arduous process that was complicated by damaging floods, stiff competition, and the death, by typhoid fever, of the system's principal engineer, Thomas Oakes. When the canal finally opened on May 20, 1825, the system ran 108 miles from Reading to Philadelphia and featured, according to Harry Rinker, author of *The Schuylkill Navigation: A Photographic History,* the multitude of dams, canals, locks, and aqueducts enumerated above.

Haven

Listen:

If someone were to ask her what she wanted most, she would say,
Give me a long ride on the river. Give me a canal song to sing and a
captain to sing it with. Give me the romance of moonlight.

She pictures herself floating in from Schuylkill Haven, watching the
trees and the fish and the towns slide by. She imagines herself learning the canals well enough to name the mules, to care for coal, to tell
canalling stories of her own. *There was once a hook-armed bowsman,*
she'd begin. *There was once a woman they called Ham and Eggs who
jig-danced for every quart of whiskey. There was once a boy who hid
himself among chickens in the cabin.*

She is keen to the hidden craving in all things: the yearning tucked
inside the songs of birds, the unconfessed regrets of men, the
permanent rage of an unfinished fire. My craving the loudest of all,
for I do not wish to be diverted from myself, to be sucked down pipes
and into homes, to be severed into locks and keys, to be dammed and
forebayed and waterwheeled toward a reservoir, and out again,
through bored wooden pipes, and into the calamity of homes.

Water Wheels

From time to time I'd see her walking, slowly, down by my shore—
her to-the-ground coat pulled close across her chest in winter, an oat-
colored dress loose on her narrow shoulders come the heat. Else, I'd
catch a glimpse of her in a carriage further up, her scarf high on her
neck and her eyes averted from the man with whom she might have
been conversing. She carried books in her one hand, always books,
and she had about herself a stillness of soul that was both detached
and, to things most others could not see, decidedly devoted. I
thought of her as levitating. That's just the idea that would wash in—
the idea of levitating.

Later her coat was pale green. She rode with her husband behind two
spotted ponies and would come down to assess the reflection of the
stars, or to sit among the song of crickets. Mornings, she'd fill her
pockets with the seeds of flowers that had gone stiff in late season.
She would not study herself in my gloss, but she would take my temperature. Just as she had when she once poured me down among her
mother's violets.

After a while, I did not see her. I had been hammered into, widened,
locked down, pumped, siphoned, and the sound of the wheels was
impenetrable. I lost the thought of me, misplaced my meaning. I lost
her, among so many other things, in the fight to undrown myself.

Now it is all these years later, and yesterday one crowd was gathered
at the saloon, and another stood in the flying frizz above the dam,
and another collected before the room of my most abject torture;
thank you, Mr. Frederick Graff, for the miracle of the water wheels
that kidnap me from myself. I distracted myself with the trajectory of
a hovering dragonfly, the way I've lately taught myself to do, and
that's how I found her, standing a bit off, in the distance.

It was in the way she stood and watched me that I knew her to be her.
That I knew us both to have aged irreparably.

John Caspar Wild, *Fairmount Water Works,* 1838.
Print and Picture Collection, The Free Library of Philadelphia.

Though Latrobe had succeeded in diverting some of the Schuylkill into Philadelphia homes, pressures on the city's water supply continued to mount in the early nineteenth century. Hired by Philadelphia's Watering Committee, Frederick Graff undertook the design of a new water system that featured a Federal-style building housing two steam engines capable of extruding the river water up to a new stone-slab-lined reservoir on the top of Faire Mount. Still, the system, whose construction began in 1812, was far from fail proof. The boilers, powered by twenty cords of wood each day, were subject to frequent fits of misbehavior. They killed two engineers by force of their explosions.

Soon the city secured a deal with the Schuylkill Navigation Company that enabled it to build a dam below Faire Mount and thereby harness the potential power of the river herself. Stoppered by the dam, the river surged toward a new forebay, then was escorted, by means of wood and cast-iron water wheels, up through the mill building and into an expanded reservoir. From there the river water moved through iron mains before it was piped toward her final destinations.

By October 1822, the wheels were being powered by the dam alone. A few years later, the engine house was converted into a public saloon, and increasing numbers of city dwellers and visitors were making their way to the Water Works to gain an unparalleled view of both the river and the machinery that had enslaved her.

Meteors above the Colossus

In the early part of the evening she held the lantern out ahead, lighting her way. She stopped for a while by a knoll, sitting on a bench, dropping her head back to watch the skies. Her coat was that shade of red that beneath the moon seems blue, except for where the lantern turned it ginger.

Others had been about, but now as she began walking again it was later and the cold had set in. When she turned onto the bridge, the wind blustered, then calmed. She didn't stop walking until she'd reached the middle of the bridge, where the single arch peaks and the moon, I imagine, is well reflected by my waters. She planted the lantern by her boots. She leaned as far as a woman could.

The way she stood on the bridge, the lantern casting color up toward her chin, she seemed a portrait, framed and changed by the years she'd waited for a night like this, alone. Sometimes a carriage rattled past. Sometimes a young man with his hands in his pockets, scuttling away from some mischief, or a loose dog, or a cat. An owl went up and down and up with a mouse in the cradle of its talons. A mole dashed and hid. Something wheezed and something barked. A leaf still on a tree broke away and skidded off into the dark.

I don't know what time the stars began to fall. Began to pitch themselves straight out of the skies, as if someone were tossing spears of light or putting a spark to a dried thatch of hay, as if it were the beginning of time, all over again. But star after star crumbled, and who can say if it was by accident or by fate or by love that the lantern she had placed by her feet at the bridge spilled and fell. Broke me apart. Burned me through.

And here it still sits now, its glow washed out.

W. H. Bartlett, *Schuylkill Water Works,* 1839.
Print and Picture Collection, The Free Library of Philadelphia.

Philadelphia would continue to earn international acclaim for its bridges, with many remarkable examples sometimes occupying a single site over time. The Wernwag Bridge, which had helped facilitate the transportation of agricultural products and livestock across the river since its construction in 1812, had earned the appellation Colossus, for the 340-foot wooden span was supported by no intermediate piers. When fire destroyed it in 1838, it was replaced by the Wire Bridge, one of the earliest suspension bridges in the world. In 1875, the Wire Bridge was superseded by a double-decker bridge, designed to astonish (and transport) the Centennial crowds. It too would vanish from the skyline, however, to be replaced by the present Spring Garden Street Bridge in the mid-twentieth century in an effort to accommodate the Schuylkill Expressway.

On November, 13, 1833, the skies above the Colossus would have seemed richly alive: "A beholder says, he was sitting alone in a well lighted apartment at 4 AM, when he suddenly saw through the window a shower of sparks falling past it on the outside," reports *Watson's Annals.* "He supposed the house was on fire, and rushing to the door, to his extreme amazement, he found the entire atmosphere filled with flakes of fire, (for they fully resembled flakes of snow of a stellated or radiated form) of a pale rose red, seemingly of an inch diameter, falling in a vertical direction, as thick as he ever saw snow! Intermingled with the smaller stars were a larger kind, equal to one in a hundred of the others, of an intense sapphire blue, seemingly of three to four inches diameter."

Love

From possibly beyond the three clustered chestnut trees, a bird calls. It's early, dawn, and besides this first sweet tremor, it is strangely quiet, and I wonder if I have been sleeping.

Now the first bird bleats, and a second answers. And now it goes on like this: bleating and rustling, then silence. Most of the birdsong is the nothing within the song. Most of the quiet is this stretch before the sea, the turtles feigning nonchalance, the mussels holding their gossip within their razored lips.

There is gold above my surface that rises now, to pink.

Eden

They have remade me in their image and called my beauty primal.

The Water Works and its bucolic surround drew the attention of visitors from around the world and continued to gain popularity among the locals. Diaries and journals were filled with the musings of inspired passersby. Passages in books exclaimed the Schuylkill's beauty. Charles Dickens, Mark Twain, and many others would eventually immortalize the place with their poetic or wry observations.

In 1835, one year after her (ultimately disastrous) marriage to Pierce Butler, a wealthy slave-owner from Philadelphia, the British-born actress, writer, and abolitionist Fanny Kemble was moved to write in her journal about the river: "It was more like a lake, just here, than a flowing stream. . . . The golden sky, the mingled green, brown, yellow, crimson, and dark maroon, that clothed the thickets; the masses of grey granite, with the vivid mossy green that clung round them; the sunny purple waters; the warm, red colour of the road itself, as it wound down below, with a border of fresh-looking turf on either side." Quoted in Philip Stevick's *Imagining Philadelphia.*

Asylum

Sometimes an old pensioner will come down to the shore and start singing some song from his youth. And the song will be about waves and whales and a fifty-foot serpent and women, especially women. And he'll be a hobbled man, so he'll have a cane, and he'll smell more like smoke than good breeding, and his lips will be pale and chewed into; his nose will have been burnished by the sun. The songs will come out of the barrel of his chest. His stories will be for nobody but me.

I'm all for that. I'm all for any story a man might relinquish, for any variety of serenade. Just take me to the sea. Just show me how it's done.

Once the country estate of a wealthy Philadelphia family, The Plantation at Gray's Ferry became home to the U.S. Naval Asylum in the early nineteenth century. Designed by William Strickland, the complex was heralded as one of the greatest examples of Greek Revival architecture in the country and featured individual rooms for disabled seamen, a hospital, and sweeping views of the Schuylkill and rural countryside. Between 1839 and 1845, the complex also served as home to the U.S. Naval Academy, until crowded conditions forced the academy's relocation to Annapolis. A few years after construction of the Naval Asylum was complete, another critical Philadelphia institution—the Blockley Almshouse—rose on the opposite shore, on land formerly owned by the Hamilton family.

John Caspar Wild, *Alms House*, 1838. Print and Picture Collection,
The Free Library of Philadelphia.

Anthracite

The man could sing, and he was a big man, so his voice went far.
He had two mules—Betty and Lou—that pulled him along. He'd
leave his wife and two children in Pottsville and pick up Annie at
Norristown—still singing, hardly changing his tune, guilt not affecting
the direction of his song, because it was like that when the coaling
started. When the men began calling heaps of floating anthracite
home, and made family along the river to keep from being lonely.

Annie went for the moonlight. Woke up past noon, when the man
was already singing, heightened the flame on the tea in the pot,
straightened out the tablecloth, and if it was May, sometimes, or if it
was April, she'd lie belly down on the barge after drinking her tea,
and watch herself doing no more than watching me.

He'd change the words to his songs when he knew she was listening.
He'd rattle two spoons against the shell of his knee and pick up the
tempo, and though she was getting on in years, she'd get to her feet
and begin to dance when his music reached a certain tempo.

"Come on, Annie," he'd say.

And she'd say, "Darling."

Though the discovery of anthracite in the valleys north of the city gave prospectors hope as
early as 1792, it wasn't until the 1820s that coal became a valued commodity and coal barges
a common sight on the Schuylkill River. In 1825, according to Edwin Wolf's *Philadelphia:
Portrait of an American City*, 5,000 tons of coal were shipped down the canal. By 1841, that
tonnage had reached 584,692. By 1845, the railroads were giving the river stiff competition
as a carrier of this dark, polluting, combustible, hard, black sedimentary rock.

Fins

He could not have been more than sixteen, and he'd either lost his shoes or never had any. He'd come from the sound of sticks and stones, and in advance of the mobbing coal-heavers, up on the shore, who were destroying whatever black thing they could find, whichever black somebody could not run fast enough to take cover in Mr. Dewey's storehouse at the wharf at Walnut Street. The coal-heavers wearing red flannel and check shirts. The officers wearing green in the buttonholes of their coats.

The boy running. The boy holding one of his arms with the sling of the other, his shadow out ahead of him, skinny, dark as he was, and wounded. Oh, Missus, addressing me. Oh, Missus, as if I had the arms to hold him, a needle and thread to stitch in a seam where the club had broken his skin apart.

Only fear runs a boy like he ran, and, probably, pain. Probably the stain of the blood on his sleeve, his wanting to get clean of the chaos, but—see?—the boy couldn't swim. He pulled his knees to his chin and threw himself deep, and then he could not stand, nor breathe.

I wanted to say, Stay calm. I wanted to say, I will buoy you down-stream, and—every swimming, flying thing as my witness—this I did. In a haze of dragonflies, above the backs of turtles, I finned him south, delivering him to the banks where he could stand and walk again. So that he might take his torn arm home, where perhaps the white men would forget to find him.

At a Schuylkill coal yard on August 2, 1842, Irish workers raged against the blacks. The riot would not cease until it had spread east to Moyamensing and was suppressed by militia.

Heroes

Like ladies at tea the girls circled close at their mothers' feet, cooling each other with the fallen leaves of tulip trees and nibbling at fried chicken. Their brothers were among those netting and freeing the big-winged butterflies, and their older sisters had gone down toward the shadows of the tall pine trees in their sherbet-colored dresses. It was Sunday afternoon at Lemon Hill. The smell of lit-up cigars emanated from the saloon. Two mop-haired boys had begun to tap in wickets for another game of croquet, and all along the carved-out paths, men and women walked decorously, or stood beside their horses, laughing.

Unnoticed at first, a pram had started down the hill. Perhaps the child's mother had neglected to brake its front wheel, perhaps a dog running past had dislodged it, but the pram had almost imperceptibly wheeled away from its place beneath the tree, then accelerated as if struck by sudden ambition. Maneuvering then over the full face of a rock, over a bald patch in the hill, over tree roots, tipping slightly as it nicked an abandoned parasol, it regained its balance and pitched forward, choosing a path beneath the branches of low trees.

By then it was as if someone had tossed bright streamers across the hill—as if a switch had been flipped on the day, catapulting cousins, sisters, friends, lovers, men, mop-haired boys down the slope, across the paths, between the trees, sending musicians flying, even the waitress from the saloon had tossed off her boots and was flying, and also hats and wickets and fried chicken wings, and in all of this commotion, somehow, was the baby's mother, who had gone off to get ice cream and had returned to the nightmare of her own baby's pram rushing wildly for me.

But the pram clattered into a tree before it ever got close to my edge. Struck an old pine face-forward, so that all of its propulsion whiplashed back instantaneously. The pram stalled long enough for the crowd finally to reach it, for someone—a boy, I think, or a young man—to lean in and collect the child, to hold her aloft so that the others might see that the chase had come to no more than this, that the day might go on as it had been going on, with the end of so many meals, the start of croquet.

W. H. Bartlett, *Fairmount Gardens,* 1839.
Print and Picture Collection, The Free Library of Philadelphia.

After Robert Morris, a hero of the Revolutionary War and a good friend of George
Washington, was convicted and imprisoned as a debtor, his Schuylkill estate was bought at a
sheriff's sale by Henry Pratt. A merchant, Pratt turned the grounds into an even more mag-
nificent garden and replaced Morris's home with a new house that featured grand side
porches and oval rooms. In 1844, a few years after Pratt's death, the city purchased the
property as part of what would become a massive program to acquire the grounds around
the Water Works and thereby ecologically preserve the purity of the river itself; this first
purchase represented the very beginnings of Fairmount Park. With its saloon and music
stand, its seductive ravines and paths, its beds of wildflowers, forsythia, spirea, and lilac,
and its gigantic tulip trees and pines, Lemon Hill ultimately became the site of many a picnic
and adventure.

Waste

Nothing would stay in its place; nothing was fixed. The bulbs of the
trees, the piers, the docks, the locks, and the canal masters' houses,
the soft hats and vests of the masters, their dinner plates and table-
cloths, the barges, the names of the barges, the Conshohocken
Bridge and the Flat Rock Bridge, the keys that opened the doors to
the mills, the mills, the equipment in the mills, the columns of smoke
that puffed out of the mills, the white lead and bark and plaster, the
bottles of medicine, the crates of live chickens, the cracked whiskey
barrels, the baskets of candles, the hammer, the nail, and the saw
someone had hung over a hook in a tool shed, the tool shed, the
hook, a pair of abandoned eyeglasses, a jar of coins, one saturated
slipper, the frame and tail of a child's kite, the stalks of flowers turning to seeds, and everything mud-colored and torn or broken, everything, once split apart, a weapon, a further means of further annihi-
lation, a beating like I have never taken.

I swallowed their folly down. I became the hell they'd predicated.
Their corpses lay sludged on my bottom. Their perfectly ruined,
wasted things.

On September 2, 1850, torrential rains swept down the largely deforested banks and
engorged the river—uprooting foundations, dismantling bridges, dislodging dams, and
destroying mills and homes at drowning speed. Much of the tediously built canal system
was shattered, necessitating a massive rebuilding program. Nineteen years later, on
October 4, 1869, the river would again be besieged by a massive storm that would again
demonstrate the vulnerability of an environment razed and reshaped according to the
pressures of development.

Civil War

They leave in a rumble on the bridges overhead, their hopes carried in their pockets, their pin-pricked women in the factories, there, or in the vegetable stalls at the market, or at home, already watching through windows.

The air is strange afterwards, crinkled with foreboding.

I should not be the only one who remembers what war does.

By 1860 there were more than half a million Philadelphians. With a quiltwork of ethnic populations and the largest black population of any northern state, the Quaker City was famously diverse, if not entirely tolerant of racial differences. It was poised right above the Mason-Dixon line, with countless profitable business ties to the southern states. The outbreak of the hostilities that would become the Civil War put the city on edge.

Eventually some 90,000 Philadelphians would enlist in the Union's cause. New hospitals would be built to take in the wounded. And many of the gray-blue uniforms of Union soldiers would be stitched by some 10,000 Philadelphia seamstresses and tailors and stored in the Schuylkill Arsenal, a complex of warehouse and manufacturing facilities that had been built along the river near Gray's Ferry some six decades before.

Respects

He must have climbed up into a tree and shimmied out across a limb
and snapped a blooming branch with his one strong arm, then
climbed back down and come up from the south of the city, to see
me. He was dressed respectfully in black, his trousers cinched in
tight to his waist with a thick rope belt and his war canteen close over
one pocket. He wore a Union cap—his own or somebody else's.

The bells had pealed so long they'd become the weather, and the
horses that had passed—with riders in their saddles or carriages
dragged behind them—had been keeping their heads low. The
wharves had been blackened, and also the boats, and there were
bolts of black unfurled from the windows in the buildings all up and
down my banks. Above the dam, where spring had already set in,
the bushes and the birds were somber. The machines, for the most
part, had stopped—the ambush of noise from factories.

Fifteen years is a war later and a very long time, and his face had
grown into itself. He took up the silence beside me and prayed.
I found him—how should I put this?—dignified. When finally he
bent and, one by one, set the magnolia buds to drift upon my surface,
I studied the emotion in his eyes so that I might remember it, think
of it later when I would seek my own redemption.

"In honor," he said.

A white flotilla on the blackest day.

When news of the fall of Richmond came on April 10, 1865, Philadelphians were ecstatic—
ringing the bell at Independence Hall, careening off into parades, breaking into song, firing
off a cannon from the roof of the *Evening Bulletin* building. A war that had extracted
unimaginable losses had finally come to its end.

But just five days later, on April 15, an altogether different sort of message reached the
city: President Lincoln was dead at the hands of an assassin. Draping its buildings in black,
tolling the bells of mourning, Philadelphians received their president on Saturday, April 22, in a
solemn ceremony.

Sculling

The Quaker Cities wear trefoils on their collars. The Universities are red and black stripes. Bachelors are bright in blue flannel and gilt buttons. Philadelphias prefer double-breasted shirts.

It is the end of March. They are returned. They have carried their shells out to their respective docks, their rowing suits and flags, their oars, and, amidst much talking and sometimes whistling, they have made them good again. Darning wherever the moths have been, repairing any nicks or dents, sliding the flags back into the staffs, working with the grain of the oars, so that they might launch like slippers.

They will be miraculously quiet. They will glide toward morning, and toward bridges, and often a tooth of the moon will still be hanging in the sky, or the rising sun won't have yet assumed its shape, and it'll be just breathing and oar, breathing and oar, small displacements generating speed. And a baby girl on the banks in her father's arms will watch the scullers sculling by. "Katherine," her father will say, and she'll point her finger.

Despite the industrialization of the lower river and the commotion of the mills further north, the damming of the Schuylkill at the Water Works in 1822 had created, as far as the Falls, an undisturbed calm—a body of water nestled in a parklike setting that soon became famous among oarsmen nationwide. Boat racing on the river began in 1835, the "Schuylkill Boat Song" was published in 1842, and with the founding of the Schuylkill Navy in 1858, regattas became a common sight. In 1869, the *Hiawatha* of the Malta Club was recorded as rowing the three-mile racing distance in 18 minutes and 2 seconds. In 1876, the Schuylkill hosted the world's first international regatta.

Anthracite

I hate the color of it. I hate the weight of it upon my back. I hate its tumorous feel, its cancerous creep along my shoals, the mess it leaves between the gills of fish, its fatal insensitivities.

I move like a black snake through a hostile landscape of reconfiguring things. Among wharves and the boats that tie themselves up to wharves. Among factories and output.

An alien to myself, increasingly.

The anthracite mines in Schuylkill County would become the leading producers of coal in the United States. By the middle of the nineteenth century, Philadelphia was firmly established as a manufacturing center, with forges and coal-fueled factories all up and down the river. Above Fairmount Park and along the lower river, smoke poured out of chimneystacks. Wheels were powered with river water. Noise from the factories—for textiles, hats, glass, medicines, paints, gas pipes, locomotives, fittings, dyes, and paper products—was omnipresent. Below the dam, the riverbanks were overtaken by coal wharves and yards, while the river herself grew ever more clotted with accumulating deposits of coal silt.

Lock attendants, 1895. Philadelphia Water Department Historical Collection.

Nostalgia

Every now and then the music will pour down from George's Hill, as if the musicians are sitting high in the hemlock trees and performing for the birds. Someone sitting on a steamboat or walking along the west canal will remember Bobby Arnold's Tavern and the catfish that it served, the rum punches and mint juleps, waffles they'd spend a month dreaming of, and not only that, but how, after a long nap following a big meal, they'd all go swimming nude.

And then the storytellers will get around to old Godfrey Schronk and his blessed dip-net, his habit of lifting thousands of fish straight out of their schools. Black-backed catfish and perch and grown-to-fullness shad, the fishing boats latched to the rocks and the seines so heavy it took a mind of strength to lift them.

Fairmount, Philadelphia from *Appleton's Journal*, 1868. Philadelphia Water Department Historical Collection.

And someone will say, River don't give us fish like that anymore.

And I'll want to say, River's given more than you ever should have taken.

On the west side of the river, at Belmont, was a place called George's Hill, where, it is written, hemlocks grew 243 feet above the tide and a gorgeous view of the Schuylkill might be had. Belmont was the original estate of Judge William Peters. When he passed away, the estate was placed in the care of his son, Judge Richard Peters, who was famous not just for his hospitality but also for the way he sang and for the stories he told. George's Hill was incorporated into Fairmount Park in 1867 and would later become the site of the Centennial Exposition.

Steam

At this hour the night seems intoxicated, the tinted lanterns swinging to some late-shift tune and the men passing through the bilious smoke above the tracks—passing through and disappearing.

They've left on the eyes of the locomotives. They've left them breathing there—each so much bigger than a bear, so much blacker than the panther whose footprints are sunk in deep beneath those tracks, whose eyes needed only the moon for ignition.

I can no longer tell you where the owls have gone. I can't explain what a night alone is.

Locomotives continued to assert their power as the century wore on—taking an increasing share of the transportation business away from the canals, opening up new corridors to passengers, and reconfiguring the city. In 1850, new stone piers, abutments, and wing-walls were added to the Market Street Bridge so that the Columbia and Pennsylvania railroad tracks might be connected. The rail yards on the western bank of the river, meanwhile, grew ever more complex and congested.

Winter of 1872: Frozen Through

I imagine I look dead to them—all bones, no skin. Or ancient and archeological, a relic dumped out of an inconceivable past.

They come by way of sleighs that are pulled through the snow by elegant horses. They are wrapped in wool coats and animal skins.

Children are urged to touch me, to consider how closely I compare with their lettered building blocks. They squeal and they smack and with a stick they poke, except for one little girl who stands apart from it all, with something like sympathy.

One enterprising vendor has brought his roasted chestnuts to the base of the bridge and is doing a brisk business.

"Above the Skating-club house the stream was choked with blocks of ice that had been tossed about in inextricable confusion by the action of the flood, great masses being thrown up on the drive. Above Girard Avenue Bridge it was more densely packed. Above Columbia Bridge it was at its worst, for the masses there—blocks, crags, peaks—were piled high in the air, the drive thereabout being buried under these boreal fragments which had tumbled up among the trees with the wrecks of rustic bridges. It was a wild, grim rugged scene, and thousands went every day to see it." Excerpted from *A Century After: Picturesque Glimpses of Philadelphia and Pennsylvania*, edited by Edward Strahan.

Zoological Gardens

It must have been a keen sense of irony that provoked them to chain an elephant to an old oak tree, to dig cages for prairie dogs, to import monkeys and hyenas from across the seas, to clip the wings of birds. The noise is killing—the hysterical chatter and proximate screams of animals slowly being robbed of their opinion.

Last night lightning seared the underbelly of the sky and thunder moved in loud and fast. It would go from dark to a sick, pale green, then flame straight back to nothingness, and all I could think of were the cinnamon bears at the dancing poles, so far from wherever it was that they had come from. Suddenly I knew what is worse than having needs you cannot speak, and that is this: having no faith in being answered.

Philadelphia's Zoological Gardens, the nation's first such showplace for captive animals, opened in July 1874 on the west bank of the river, near the Girard Avenue Bridge. Generations before, John Penn, William Penn's literary grandson, had built his home on this site and called it Solitude; he'd spent a good deal of his time there writing poetry. The creators of the Zoo incorporated Solitude into its grounds while building new structures— The Aviary, The Eagle House, The Bear Pits, The Carnivora House—to contain the range of animals that were acquired. Admission was twenty-five cents for adults, half-price for children.

Mighty

Perhaps it is more pleasant to see the Mighty Corliss than to listen to its hiss and thunder, its shafts and pulleys—a noise I carry with me, to the great exasperation of the fish. Even the trees on the banks seem to hold their green heads back from the rumble up the hill, as if they, too, know that there is no hope for contemplation going forward.

How is it that something man has made is more spectacular than all that he will never fashion with his own hands? Birds, for instance. Clouds. The eternity of rivers.

Their temerity is killing.

On May 10, 1876, the hundredth anniversary of the founding of the nation was celebrated by the opening of the Centennial Exposition—a six-month-long extravaganza perched high above the west bank of the Schuylkill. The Centennial was blessed upon its opening by a slightly soggy President Ulysses S. Grant and attracted some 62,000 visitors each day thereafter. It offered a wide variety of exhibits, sunken gardens and spraying fountains, a grand Gothic-style Agricultural Hall, stockyards and a horse track, miniature excursions into China, Russia, and elsewhere, and the very latest in women's work and life-saving equipment. Within Machinery Hall, the defining tempo of an industrializing America was unveiled as thirteen acres of machines were powered into action by the Double Corliss Engine. Those who could not walk the fair's hundreds of acres were encouraged to make themselves comfortable in a wheeled Centennial chair. Steamboats crowded the Schuylkill throughout that spring and summer bearing eager, hopeful visitors. The International Rowing Regatta, the first-ever event of its kind, brought wider appreciation for the river's composed course.

Katherine Rows

She favors the idea of the continuous. The continuous glide. The unobstructed move through time. The going on of my own self and soul—strong as a man, she says of me, and fluid as a mother's song.

Saturdays she walks north, amidst the dust of horse-cars, the hurry of women with basketsful of peas, and the painted advertisements, to Spring Garden Street, where she turns west, toward Fairmount Bridge. At the bridge she goes south again, onto the gravel paths among the spirea and forsythia, the tulip trees with their branches hung with ladies' parasols, the sweet, deep moss. She goes past the saloon and the music stand, past the games of cricket and the men in soft gray suits, toward the standpipe and the Water Wheel—the amateur fishers with their lines hooked out for the golden carp and catfish and black bass that still swim unto me. She wears a simple navy skirt and a white cotton blouse. She wears nothing on her hands, or on her fingers.

She'd been born the year of the *Hiawatha*. Her father took her to the nationals in '73, and sat her down on the sloping hill, which she would not leave until the final shell had gone its full course. She'd gone with him on every one of the twenty-five days of the International Rowing Regatta, when the Beaverwycks conquered London and also Yale in the fours, and Ed Hanlan became famous for beating the field. A passing oarsman had shown her the medal he had won—a single scull at the coin's risen center, thirteen stars about its rim.

She can tell anyone the meaning of distance and speed: Two thousand sixty feet from Turtle Rock to the Girard Avenue Bridge. One mile and a half from Turtle Rock to Peter's Island. Two miles and two thousand three hundred feet to the landing at Laurel Hill. Two miles and four thousand six hundred feet to the Falls Bridge.

She racks her cedar scull at Vespers, among the longer shells and the other wherries, among the disassembled slides and stretchers, always something under repair, always a man studying the planking in a shaft of window light. When she walks it toward me, she wears it upside down on her head like a hat, her hands on the riggers. She rolls it over and lays it down, pulls the oars through the chokes, fastens the gates, and settles her heart. She plants her feet in the stretchers and oars her way out, her back facing forward. *Shoulders to the sky, Katherine. Knees at an angle. Catch and drive and always finish. Feather the blades so you'll fly.*

She leaves her hair loose, a dark burst about her face. She lets the breeze into her blouse. She listens to me and to what I have to say, and she goes and she goes and she goes toward the wirework of the Girard Avenue Bridge. Toward the ghost of John Penn and the animals that have come to town to live in their fanciful abodes: the Fox Pens, the Wolf Pens, the Raccoon House, the village for the prairie dogs, the stoned-in pits for bears, the house of birds. Toward the eagles and the lions and the rhinos, roaring and squawking in anticipation of food, and in lonesomeness for the places they'd been taken from.

Oars in, oars out. Knees to her chest and knees gone flat, and she does not vary the angle of her elbows.

A hawk has flown in from the east. Its red-tipped wings and tail now mirrored in my surface.

Intimations: Anthony Drexel

He walks from the west toward the east, alone—his collar drawn up to his ruddy chin and his thoughts wherever he keeps them. He's a man of routines, and most mornings his face seems weighted by the brown bush of his mustache, though when the light is good and the clouds are thick and pinked by the sun, something lifts in him and he pauses, however briefly, on the bridge and looks south, over the sludge I am becoming.

Evenings, he walks back, east toward west, often alone, but in his best frame of mind when he is accompanied by his friend and the talk between them is of J. P. Morgan or the day's headlines or last night's banquet for newsboys. The things hoped for and the things done, the things waiting to be done. There is a town, west, that they have begun to plan.

More and more they speak of green the way I remember green, of quiet the way I long for it, of streams that flow clean. This is how I begin to understand that the world is moving past me. That far beyond my reach Philadelphians might start again. That I may be worth abandoning.

Anthony Drexel was a financier who had worked in his father's currency brokerage house since the age of thirteen and who became, among other things, senior business partner to J. P. Morgan. George W. Childs was a book-loving clerk who, with Drexel's help, had become the publisher of Philadelphia's esteemed newspaper, the *Public Ledger*. Together these two best friends engineered the town of Wayne on a large parcel of land along the Pennsylvania Railroad's Main Line, accelerating the exodus from the city of a middle class increasingly weary of smog, noise, and the dusty heat of summer.

Winter 1902, Schuylkill River ice. Print and Picture Collection, The Free Library of Philadelphia.

Ooze

And just like that the wheels of the Water Works stop spinningspin-ningspinning, and I'm thick with myself, a viscous ooze held but not held between the walls they built to tame me. I am abiotic, the color of a bruise, a river stripped of her own enchantments, and so entirely past my beauty that I ache for what I surely must have been—lithe and limpid, a seduction and also something yearning to be seduced.

There are ghosts on the hills where the azaleas were. There are no lovers on the bridge, no poets in the moonlight, no young woman in a scull trying to fly. Though sometimes two boys will come out with scavenger ambitions, dig about in the dirty banks, and find a broken treasure.

By the mid-1880s, fouled water, factory waste, anthracite by-products, and agricultural and urban runoff were being drained into the Schuylkill at an alarming rate—killing the aquatic life, raising a stink, and endangering the "preserved" water of Fairmount Park. But it wasn't until 1909 that the city finally closed the Water Works for good and began to plan for the dismantling of the reservoir on the hill. Soon the Philadelphia Museum of Art would stand in the reservoir's place.

Schuylkill River from South Street Bridge, 1876. Philadelphia Water Department Historical Collection.

Influenza

Here is a boy pinching his coat collar up to his nose and leaving his hat smashed down hard on his head. He's come across through tall grasses, through the improvised trails, alongside rusting rails and past the docks, and still he holds his stiff wool collar up against his nose, as if that might protect him from the vapors. Something about the way he walks, with one hand to his face and the other dug deep inside his pockets, asserts his mourning. Something makes me notice him, and how deeply he is hurting.

When he comes in close, it almost seems like my suggestion. When he bends and leans forward, he finds the specter of his own masked face afloat. Finally he releases the clot of fabric at his nose and digs down deep into both coat pockets and retrieves what seem to be seven miniature sailboats. All with bright silk colors for sails and polished wood for hulls.

Each boat is different, and differently spectacular.

"Joey," the boy says, as he sets each one to sail. "Joey, Joey," seven times, and at the end of this litany of a single name he says two words: "I'm sorry."

The boy's memory set down upon the bed of my own dark, sluicing tears. Another flotilla.

By the dawning of World War I, Philadelphia was a manufacturing center—a supplier of both goods and men to the front line, a builder of ships at its famous Navy Yard, located on the Delaware at its juncture with the Schuylkill. In early January 1918, however, twenty-eight inches of snow and a coal shortage slowed many of the engines of activity, shortening work-weeks and leaving many homes cold and poorly lit. Nine months later the city was once again ravaged by an epidemic. On September 18, 1918, the first death from influenza was reported in Philadelphia; within two weeks, 4,000 were dead. South Philadelphia was the hardest hit. People walked the streets with their coat collars pulled up way past their chins.

Suppurating

It is the worst of you sloughed off into me—your refuse and oddments, your savage toxins and dross, your slicks that do not sink, your dirty yeast, your wrong-colored wools and the dyes that wronged them. How is it that I became the quickest route to your confession—the door you close to those parts of yourself that you hope no one will see?

Call me what you've made me, which is a grave. Plant me a tombstone. Hold your hands to your faces when you're near. Don't fly your kites by my shore, and do not drink me. Don't test my temperature.

Schuylkill River dump, 1924. Print and Picture Collection, The Free Library of Philadelphia.

Through ten-foot-wide pipes located on both west and east banks, early twentieth-century Philadelphians sent their sewage plunging into the river. Barges filled with domestic waste dumped their cargo along the river's shores. Paint factories, garbage-disposal plants, and other such miracles of the modern age made their awful contributions to the Schuylkill's desecration, while, near 30th Street, an oil refinery spewed and a slaughterhouse weekly flushed the offal and entrails of sheep, hogs, and cows out into a watery grave.

    Low tide and drought turned the river into a static "longitudinal cesspool," in the words of John Frederick Lewis, who further noted in his 1924 call to action, *The Redemption of the Lower Schuylkill*, "how offensive is the stench, when the air is heavy and the wind blowing from the southwest."

Revenge

Even when they have nowhere to go, they hurry past, over the
bridges, along the paths, holding their noses. The mothers hurry
their children; the men, their wives. The vendors hurry. The assorted
kitchen help looking for work at the assorted struggling hotels—they
hurry. The aimless men in their tattered suits, with their useless
briefcases. The women with their for-hire scrub brushes and buckets.
The boys playing their games of Dare. The local nuns and the col-
lared priests. The older boys with their shovels and tools, and also,
always, the apple men and their cartloads of apples and all the people
who have bought themselves an apple, who have bitten those apples
down to their cores, who think nothing of tossing the skeletons and
seeds over their turned shoulders, into me.

I dream of tendrils in my silt. Of upsurging trunks and greedy limbs.
Of tree after tree cracked wildly free from the brown slicks of seeds
that have been pitched into my wasteland. I dream myself a grove of
shaded pungency, bloomed out magisterially with gorgeous, globed
red fruit.

During the early months of the Depression, Philadelphia was only partially protected by its
diversified manufacturing economy. As the ranks of the unemployed swelled, apple-sellers
took over the streets.

Something

When the women oar in, I sense their power.

No matter what was happening on the river's lower and upper banks, the stretch between the Fairmount Dam and the Falls remained a rower's haven. Boat clubs burgeoned, regattas were held, and the course consolidated its international reputation. John B. Kelly, Sr., the Irish owner of a large brickworks, earned legendary status and brought Philadelphia Olympic gold by winning the singles and doubles title in the 1920 Games, as well as the doubles title at the 1924 Games. A few decades later, John B. Kelly, Jr., would become the nation's singles champion.

Nested between those achievements and countless others was the founding, on May 4, 1938, of the Philadelphia Girls' Rowing Club by seventeen pioneering women. Among those founders was Ernestine Bayer, a lissome, dark-haired beauty who had secretly wed an Olympic rowing champion several years before. Ernestine would soon become a champion rower in her own right and earn her place in women's sports history as the Mother of American Women's Rowing.

Last Skate

Only five of them remain, at the end of this day, in the twilight. They have been skating together all afternoon—their dark faces set off beneath their camel-colored caps, their smiles white as crescent moons, their scarves like flags. They have played catch and freeze and some bruising version of hockey, and the only girl among them has taught them to spin on two feet until they've fallen down giddy, slapping my surface with their hands.

I can't tell them what I know, which is this: There'll soon be no more skating. No more knifing in with blades. No more leaping or falling. No more leaving behind the mufflers, the scarves, the mittens, all of which I've stowed away, in my darkest, deepest water.

They can't imagine a winter without me.

Philadelphians never tired of skating on the Schuylkill. Founded on December 21, 1849, the nation's very first skating club, The Skater's Club of the City and County of Philadelphia, was organized by gentlemen determined to provide instruction both in the art of skating and in the rescue of those unfortunate souls who broke through thinly iced patches and struggled with the frosty undercurrents. Not all were saved, of course, and stories of terrifying drownings in which entire parties were swept downriver or fiancées were lost to lovers appear in Jones Wister's *Reminiscences*, among other local memoirs.

By 1863, according to a scrapbook prepared by Anne C. Lewis for her grandchildren, women had taken to the ice—attaching steel blades to their boots or deigning to sit on bladed chairs so that they might be pushed about by loved ones. A meadow along the west bank of the river at Walnut Street was fenced in and transformed into an outdoor rink, complete with a heated skate shop. A little while later, another west bank meadow, below the Gray's Ferry Bridge, was transformed into Eastwick Park, where, in Lewis's words, "skates could be hired by the hour, or repaired if broken; large rooms, well heated with huge stoves, for resting or warming oneself, a good restaurant and a fine band of music in the afternoon, and also in the evening, when it was moon-light."

The skating continued through the first part of the twentieth century, until pollutants interfered with the freezing process and the ice was no longer trustworthy.

Boathouse Row skaters. The Library Company of Philadelphia.

Abiding

You wouldn't call it survival. All that time living with what became my own stench, my insufferable loneliness. All that time, forsaken. You turned your backs on me. You robbed me of my dignity and birdsong, of fat-fisted flowers and azalea springs. Mostly you robbed me of the idea of myself as a river, for what is a river but a conduit between spring and sea, a womb for underwater things, a chance at transcendence, and what did you make of me but a trough of shame, a festering disease you would not cure? So that even the moon avoided me and my stories went dry as a bone and I was too clotted to see.

And now here you come with your dredging machines. Your scrape-away-the-filth machines. Your bring-back-the-fish machines. I abide them. I consent to being scraped into.

Hope loses its appeal.

In 1927 the Army Corps of Engineers reported that the 38 million tons of mining waste dumped, over time, into the Schuylkill had reconfigured the riverbed and provoked new flooding. The river's troubles had been further exacerbated by the clear-cutting of nearby forests. It wasn't until 1945, however, that the Schuylkill River Desilting Project was authorized—a nine-year program focused on dredging the clogged river with huge hydraulic machines and preventing further destruction, as described in a news story by Michelle Mowad. Desilting pools and impounding basins were placed up and down the shores—big concave bowls into which the wastes were collected. Factories were to use the silt as fuel. While the process itself was excruciating, it marked the beginning of the river's slow revival. Though much of the muck on the riverbed proved intransigent, the river water began to run clearer in the aftermath of the Desilting Project, enticing some back to her shore.

Dredging, 1954. Photo reprinted with the permission of the *Philadelphia Inquirer*.

Kite Tails

Years since a loose lemon would tumble down the hill.

Since the Germans played the Italian's music.

Since I could imagine myself high, on the back of a cloud.

But this morning, just ahead of a storm, there flew a kite, its tail trailing a carnival of colors through the sky.

Somewhere out there a child dares.

Falling Up

Yesterday a man came up the east bank, from the south, and did not once look back to where he'd come from. He kept walking forward, bent just a little at the hips, looking for nothing more particular, it seemed, than distance between himself and the proverbial. In the tall grasses were the season's early butterflies, and in the wake of this man's walking they rose, like falling-up confetti.

Boys were out hoping for fish. A girl was looking down at herself by looking down at me from the South Street Bridge, her flared skirt striped orange and yellow. And high above there was a hawk—so high I thought at first that it was a scrap of torn-off cloud, until it collapsed its wings and then made them wide again, availing itself of a current.

I imagined the churn of the air beneath those wings, updrafts and riffs and buoyancy. I imagined the hawk considering me and, in imagining, felt just this side of alive.

More and more, Philadelphians returned to the river's shore, looking for wings and seeds.

Jewfish: The Aquarium
at the Old Water Works

I suppose they supposed they could see their way through me—that by going down they were going deep into my aqueous philosophy. But those weren't my fish in those tanks. They were foreigners—calico, chut, roach, burr fish, croaker, Cape May goody, moonfish, porgy, skate, great tuna. They were detainees endlessly appraising the circumference of their thick glass cage, while my own fish, for their part, had long since swum far off, without me.

After a while, the sole attraction was the jewfish—that goliath grouper whose eyes always seemed too extremely small, its body perpetually on the verge of sinking. The thing never changed the dropped-jaw expression on its face; it was always (excuse me) defeated. Except for that one time, when the man from Proverbial brought his children down toward the tanks, to see. It was the man, his daughter, his son, and on the opposite side of the algaed glass, the jewfish, and something like a *frisson* passing between.

Nine years after the big wheels of the Water Works stopped turning, the old millhouse was converted into what would eventually become the fourth-largest aquarium in the world. Visitors could watch seals and sea lions flip tricks in the forebay, or they could trek down the grand staircase and stand before vast tanks of imported fish. Eventually the seals and the sea lions got sick, green algae cast an eerie hue over the tanks, and the aquarium shut its doors for good. The John B. Kelly Practice Pool would subsequently provide recreation at that site until it, too, was no longer tenable.

Comet

Every night now the comet falls, a little bit high and to the west and trailing not just yellow vapors, but a strange, impatient whisk. They have christened the comet with a name, and that name is Traffic.

The moon, meanwhile, stays in the sky. The lights of the city glow, then blaze, then die. Beneath my bridges men come to sleep, to dream water passing by.

More than twenty years after it was first proposed, the Schuylkill Expressway opened to traffic in September 1954. Decried by environmentalists, resisted by surrounding communities, and provoking the ire of West Philadelphia institutions, the Expressway presented enormous challenges to its succession of designers. Among them was the need to fit the four-lane highway into the too-small swatch of ground between the switching yards of the Pennsylvania Railroad at 30th Street Station and the river itself. This obstacle was finally overcome when the engineers physically moved the west bank of the river eight feet by sinking piles into the riverbed. By the time the Expressway was unveiled, it was already inadequate for its purpose.

Flow

Little by little they return—swim, float, crawl across and through.
I do my feeble best to run cleaner. I seek to accommodate their curiosity about my museum of broken things. This arrowhead. That stovepipe hat. This jangle of gaskets and this animal rib. This triangle of a silken sail and this better half of a fractured oar, and all these window casements, light bulbs, spoons, bracelets, barrels, cartridges.

The turtles, especially, are surveyors, crawling in and out of the forsaken as if they might just hope to haul it all home under their hoods. The fish are more pugnacious, battling for the shady coves, the interiors of pipes, the hollows of empty caskets. In self-preserving hordes the insects hover.

I am inclined to feel my age. To quiet the entire ruckus come noon. To cry out in the only language I have ever known, which is flow. I had thought I wanted youth again, beauty, the powers of seduction. But in the rattle of return I feel oddly fevered, claustrophobic.

"Philadelphia," John Gunther wrote in 1951, "drinks its own sewage." It was a withering accusation, a charge that could only be dispelled over time, as a number of local and federal environmental programs were finally put into place. With the support of federal funding, the Philadelphia Water Department was able, in 1957, to employ primary wastewater treatment at all of its plants. The Clean Water Act of 1972 placed strict federal controls on point-source pollution. Then, in 1978, the Schuylkill was designated the first Pennsylvania Scenic River, initiating the removal of dams, the construction of fish ladders, and the reintroduction of American shad in the lower river. A few years later, Philadelphia's primary wastewater treatment program was supplemented with biological techniques. The environmental controls, regulations, and activism worked, as the river slowly became home again to numerous species of fish. Gunther's *Inside U.S.A.* is excerpted in Stevick's *Imagining Philadelphia*.

Pussy Willows

She was slim, with dark, tousled hair. He was pale. She wore long earrings. His sneakers were black. She carried a camera slung about her neck, insouciantly, as if that were the fashion. She had the habit of preoccupation—of walking ahead until he'd call her back with some bit of news, some laughable something.

The sky was their screen. They'd enter the picture at the South Street Bridge, then pass straight through it, then return, and I'd tell myself the story of all that must have happened in between. I imagined the nature of the books he carried home. I imagined the pictures in her camera.

In November it was cold. They came out together and walked together, buried their hands in their pockets.

In December the winds kicked in. Big blasting gusts of defiant air across the bridge, and below it. They wrapped their necks in woolens. Their words escaped as ice.

In January there was too much snow. In January it was brutal.

In February they walked the bridge in a hurry.

In March they did not cross the bridge at all. In March they were altogether gone, and I told myself the story of all that must have happened in between.

In April there were pussy willows in bloom along my shore. The soft white paws of spring.

From "Leaving the Temple in Nîmes," by James Wright:

And I will send one ivy leaf, green in winter,
Home to an American girl I know.
I caught a glimpse of her once in a dream,
Shaking out her dark and adventurous hair.
She revealed only a little of her face
Through the armful of pussy willow she gathered
Alive in spring,
Alive along the Schuylkill in Philadelphia.

Hurricane Agnes

So I knocked you off your feet. So I took a look around, inside your basements, your first floors. So I went off, like a thief, with your June gardens. So I rose and you couldn't stop me, so I was brown and you hate brown. So there was mud, and for weeks afterwards.

Think of this: I was kicking off your trash, spreading my wings. I was ridding myself of the insidious rats—their eyes like lights I couldn't see through.

In late June 1972, a tropical disturbance off the coast of the Yucatan Peninsula began to work its way north, becoming a hurricane by the time it reached Florida and gaining strength over the Atlantic before wending its way back toward the Northeast and precipitating, in Philadelphia, hundred-year-flood conditions. Over several days and nights the rain fell hard, ripping the underwater river cable at the Fairmount Dam and necessitating manual measurements of the river's surging height.

Dick Roy, an employee of the Philadelphia Water Department, served his stint at the river's side from midnight on a Friday through 8 a.m. the next day, calling in the river's height every fifteen minutes. Deep into that long night, he says, gunshots erupted along the Schuylkill's west bank. Casting his half-mile flashlight out along the banks, he soon discerned the source of the trouble: Rats, drowned out of their burrows by raging floodwaters, were drawing the fire of Philadelphia's police force. In 1992, Dick Roy would be named the Deputy in Charge of Operations for the Philadelphia Water Department, following many years spent overseeing the design and construction of the river's wastewater plants.

Renditions

He settles the legs of his easel into the dirt, fixes his canvas upright, mingles his tints, and tests one brush, then another. Patient as a hawk, he waits. As if I might, or could, romance my own portrait—summon loveliness for immortality's sake.

But the clouds move at their own pace, and the sun asserts itself or it does not, and I am my age, the color of the years gone by. I am fish bones and car parts, the eye sockets of muskrats, a library card and a checkbook, the broken metal plate of an old gas grill, a hammer, some nails, a tool belt, the click of whelk, an arrowhead, the dull gray of an expended bullet. I am stones and silt. Trust me.

Still, he waits. Still, every day he comes and works the legs of that easel into the skin of that earth. If I could dance for him, I would rumba. If I could turn my surface into sequins, I would shimmy by.

Even before the Water Works turned her into a favorite subject, the Schuylkill was having her portrait rendered by well-known painters and engravers. Today the Schuylkill's story can be traced through the works of artists such as William Russell Birch and his son Thomas Birch, William Groombridge, Augustus Köllner, Edmund Darch Lewis, Titian Ramsay Peale, Carl Philipp Weber, Thomas Eakins, and Patrick Connors.

Proverbial

It was her father who taught her to look for ghosts—for the rub of history and the recovered pattern. It was as if he believed one could see things through to their beginnings, as if buildings and bridges and even rivers had souls. Kites tangled in trees. Fish and birds. A floating saucer. All, as he told her, souled. He bought her her first camera so that she might fix a moment and study it afterwards. He bought her a journal and a pen she had to dip into ink. "Write it down," he told her. "Find the words."

He was a man who walked. A man who came to me and knelt by my banks so that he might come home with some bit of stone, some nest fallen from a tree, some old teacup still all in one piece, and he'd say, "Be careful, Ellen. This is history." He slipped found feathers into envelopes. He filled his pockets with skulls and beaks that had been sunbleached into ivory.

Now it is autumn, and dusk, and the skies are a purple cleaved by red, and it is his moving steadily forward that remains. The way he antici-pates possibilities. He tells her about birds and the songs birds will sing. She tells him about her photographs, about how it is the instant after you motivate the shutter that the truth comes into view. Everything lies just ahead. The days repeat, but never completely. *What if* is never *what was*. And weather is a smell.

He removes his hat so that she might take his portrait.

"The moon is on its way," he says.

Something

Every spring she was still here, slipping her oars into me. Her dark hair had gone magnificently white, and her body was still lissome. She rowed in an ocean shell, as fast as she wanted and then as slowly, looking out about her and eating her lunch, then rowing at her own pace again. She was nearing ninety, and her eyes were what I wanted to be seen with.

But yesterday her eyes were clouded, and her boat was long and flagged at both ends. There were others with her—a man, her daughter —and the box of her husband's ashes was at her feet.

I made myself still. I bent the falling rays of the sun into a mindful purple. I opened my heart to take in some of hers. It was all I had to give. It was something.

Ernestine Bayer continued to row the Schuylkill and to compete in regattas around the world even as she approached her nineties. In 1997, she spread her husband's ashes in the river.

Catfish

How they sit all day talking—boys straight up through old men. With their lines baited and sunk in, and their stories traveling all the way and back from Vietnam to Korea to a woman's apple pie. They talk fish, mostly—walleye, smallies, catfish—and they talk Zara Spooks and Spinnerbaits, Texas-style worms and pumpkin seed. They say, *Watch me walk the dog. I've had a morning full of fish strike. Look this way for snap. Damn this sticky drag. I told my missus that I was going to church. She said I should go catch her fry.*

They say fishing in daytime is like nothing compared with fishing at night. They measure out the moon with their arms and, next, the size of their haul. They talk about stripers busting on small bait and flies that push the water and muskies no less long than thirty-five inches and the trout they didn't see coming. They say you're best off plunking for shad directly alongside the quickest current, and if you want results, don't barb your lure.

If only old Godfrey Schronk could hear them now. The things they would not boast of.

In 1999, American shad were returned to the river by virtue of an intensive restocking program conducted by the Pennsylvania Fish and Boat Commission. Breaching some of the old canal dams and putting new or newly modernized fish ladders into place at both the Fairmount and Flat Rock dams made the waterways increasingly hospitable to striped bass, catfish, bottom-feeding hogsuckers, perch, sunfish, tiger muskellunge, walleyes, small- and largemouth bass, eels, and, of course, shad.

South Street Bridge Suicide

When she fell she kept her naked feet beneath her and her arms pulled tight across her chest, a portfolio of poems pressed to her heart. The sky was her screen. Her slightly wintered hair was unbound. It was somewhere between dark and dusk, and everything she wore was white. Even if I'd known, or somehow suspected, her intention, I could not have broken her fall.

I could not have saved her.

Her neck snapped, just like that, in an instant.

Her hair floated out from all around her head, like a dark gloss skimmed off the sky. Her arms unclasped and her poems dispersed, and then they blurred and sank. Her white became transparent. Her skin showed straight through to her bones. She wore a strand of pussy willows around one ankle and no other jewelry, none at all.

Sweetheart, I told her.

But, sweetheart.

Among the many things that have been dropped, thrown, lost, and forfeited to the bottom of the Schuylkill River are those who have decided to end their lives with a plunging leap from a city bridge.

Ernesta Drinker Ballard

Were I to have lived like one of you—had I a birthing and a dying,
had I the privilege of persuasion, had I a finite shape and course—
I would have lived like Ernesta, sculpting time with a purpose.

I would have seen beyond myself.

I would have reached past.

Born to privilege in 1920, Ernesta Drinker Ballard brought an indefatigable mix of optimism,
vision, and determination to her extraordinary life. In 1968, she would help found the
Philadelphia branch of the National Organization for Women. As president of the
Pennsylvania Horticultural Society, she would bring new vitality to the Philadelphia Flower
Show and bring community gardens to urban neighborhoods. And as a member of the
Fairmount Park Commission, she, together with the women she inspired, would wage a
relentless campaign to restore the Water Works to its former iconic place within the city.

Blaze

All those years the songs had stopped there, on their way to the sea. The boy singing for his mother, the soldiers singing for courage, the sailor singing to be telling, the birds courting, the coal man wanting Annie, the boys hoping for turtles, the stars imprinting their verses onto me. The sounds of the songs would get just that far and no further. They'd enter the realm of the asylum.

So that last night, when the fire broke out in that old graffiti-covered building, the songs broke with it—cacophonous, bittersweet, tragic, accusing, and, in the oddest way, consoling. Every song fit inside another song. Every lyric was, in the end, mere smoke—the ephemera of yearning, the tender afterglow of hope.

The way my heart cracked open.

On February 3, 2003, the skies above the U.S. Naval Home (formerly the Naval Asylum) burst into flames. After serving pensioners through 1976, the historic building at the southernmost tip of the Schuylkill had been abandoned. Arson was blamed for the five-alarm blaze. Subsequently, the complex would be converted into luxury townhouses.

Love

He was the most beautiful thing I had ever seen, with his dark pelt and his well-groomed ears, the sterling glimmer of his whiskers. He was audacious, bold, spectacularly witty, and when he looked at me he was looking into me, he was knowing my heart and all the places it has been to. He was not afraid of my complicated language, not afraid of my needs, not afraid of all that sinks or floats or ends with me. The bones in me, which are also seeds. The dust of distant life. The stories I carry, the color of my dreams, the weight of my confessions.

What does it matter where he's come from? The point is: He might have kept going from river to river, but he came here, to me. He has made us his secret, given me his wide soul to keep. He has told me his stories, and in that way he has saved me from my own. He has found a stone, and it's a jewel, and he has brought it to me. I tuck it into a shell.

Maybe you have to stop looking to find your one true love.

Maybe you have to trust that he'll find you.

Not long before midnight, on March 20, 2005, a river otter made its way up the Schuylkill River toward the viewing window of the fish ladder near the Art Museum. An underwater camera recorded his arrival before he slipped out of view.

Boathouse Row. Photograph by the author.

ACKNOWLEDGMENTS

The idea to write an autobiography of Philadelphia's Schuylkill River had many antecedents—my passion for the city that I have always called my own; my abiding curiosity about a river that I had, over the course of many years, walked over and beside; and my tremendous admiration for the environmentalists, businesspeople, and cultural and civic leaders who have brought their talents and vision to the river's ongoing renaissance. It has taken almost a century to relieve the river of the burdens we placed upon her. Among those who are seeing the renaissance through, I am particularly indebted to Jerry Sweeney of the Schuylkill River Development Corporation, a visionary of the first order and a friend. In addition, thanks to Louise Turan, formerly of SRDC, Kurt Zwikl of the Schuylkill River Greenway Association, Bill Lefevre of Bartram's Garden, Regina Thomas of Women for the Water Works, Ed Grusheski of the Philadelphia Water Department, Dick Roy, formerly of the Philadelphia Water Department, and Chari Towne of Schuylkill Programs, Delaware Riverkeeper Network—all of whom provided insights and support throughout the project.

Generous funding from the Pew Fellowships in the Arts enabled me to pursue my vision—to spend time experimenting with form and possibilities. Long conversations with Laura Geringer made me think harder. Days spent hunting down old texts with Moira Moody infused the book with unexpected details and enriched the process immeasurably. Thanks to Eileen Neff for sharing her memories of the jewfish. For a marvelously instructive conversation at the Fairmount Water Works Interpretive Center, and for subsequent generous help during fact checking, I am deeply grateful to Drew Brown, manager of public education for the Philadelphia Water Department. For additional support throughout the fact-checking process, I thank Frederic Ballard Jr., Joel Fry, and Katherine Wilson. Thanks as always to the indispensable Karen Lightner and Ted Cavanagh of the Free Library of Philadelphia. Many thanks as well to Patrick Connors, for permission to use the painting that graces the cover of this book, and for a memorable conversation. Thanks to Christine Poole of the remarkable Schwarz Gallery for assistance in tracking down some of the gorgeous river images the gallery has represented over time. Thanks to the Library Company for hunting down the photograph of the Boathouse Row skaters. Finally, for his help in locating and identifying many of the images that adorn these pages, I am enormously indebted to Adam Levine, who, among many other roles, serves as the archivist for the Philadelphia Water Department and possesses an encyclopedic knowledge of Philadelphia's waterways, not to mention a steadfast passion for them.

Amy Rennert, my agent, read some of the earliest drafts of *Flow* and wholeheartedly believed; her faith in these pages provided a raft to float on. Micah Kleit, my editor at Temple University Press, has made the dream of this book a reality and given it the finest possible home; for his enthusiasm, optimism, energy, and support I am eternally grateful. Likewise, Gary Kramer's embrace of the project has been extraordinary, and Jane Barry's copyediting has been both thorough and kind. Thanks, too, to Charles Ault for overseeing the book's production and to Phillip Unetic for its design and typesetting.

My friends continue to see me through. Thanks to Ivy Goodman for reading first and responding with such articulate intelligence; to Sy Montgomery, for embracing the river as a "she"; to Jennie Nash, for sending her California sun my way, always; to Alyson Hagy, for the conversations; to Reiko Rizzuto and Kate Moses, for the journey forward.

I wish to thank my parents, for the extraordinary examples they have set with their own lives, and for their love. Gratitude as always to my husband, William Sulit, this time for his help in finding Grandma Lewis's skating stories. Finally, Jeremy: Thank you for the exquisite imagination that you brought to these pages, for the inspiration of your own well-crafted stories, and for the joy you bring me, daily.

Banks, William Bennett. "Picturesque Philadelphia." *Munsey's Magazine* (December 6, 1891): 251–65.

"'Beautifully Situated on the River Schuylkill': Views of the U.S. Naval Asylum and Hospital, Philadelphia." Philadelphia Area Consortium of Special Collections Libraries (PACSCL). http://www.pacscl.org/shows/navalhome/index.html.

Brookhouser, Frank. *Our Philadelphia: A Candid and Colorful Portrait of a Great City.* New York: Doubleday & Co., 1957.

Chambers, William. *Things As They Are in America.* Philadelphia: Lippincott, Grambo, 1854.

Columbian Magazine 3 (May 1789): 282–83. "George Washington, First Inauguration, April 30, 1789." Library of Congress American Memory website, "I Do Solemnly Swear . . . : Presidential Inaugurations." http://international.loc.gov/ammem/pihtml/piwio1.html.

"Continuation of the Excitement." *Daily Chronicle and General Advertiser* (August 3, 1842).

Davis, Rebecca Harding. "A Glimpse of Philadelphia in July 1776." *Lippincott's Magazine* 52 (July 18, 1876): 27.

———."Old Philadelphia." *Harper's Monthly* 52 (April 1876): 705–21; (May 1876): 868–82.

Delaware Riverkeeper Network. "The Piedmont Delaware River Basin." http://www.delawareriverkeeper.org/theriver/piedmont.asp.

Driver, Clive E., ed. *Passing Through: Letters and Documents Written in Philadelphia by Famous Visitors.* Philadelphia: Rosenbach Museum, 1982.

DuBois, W. E. B. *The Philadelphia Negro: A Social Study.* 1899; reprint, Philadelphia: University of Pennsylvania Press, 1999.

Faris, John T. *The Romance of Old Philadelphia.* Philadelphia: Lippincott, 1918.

Federal Writers' Project. *WPA Guide to Philadelphia.* Philadelphia: University of Pennsylvania Press, 1988.

Finkel, Kenneth. "Marking Pennsylvania History: The Horses That Saved America." http://www.whyy.org/91FM/marker_mifflin.html.

"Fort Mifflin: The Only Fort in Philadelphia." http://www.fieldtrip.com/pa/54923395.htm.

Gibson, Jane Mork. "The Fairmount Water Works." Philadelphia Museum of Art *Bulletin* 84, nos. 360–61 (Summer 1988). Online version: Philadelphia Water Department website: http://phillyh2o.org./backpages/PMA_TEXT.htm.

Levine, Adam. "The History of Philadelphia's Watersheds and Sewers." Philadelphia Water Department website: http://www.phillyh2o.org/.

Lewis, Anne C. "Scrapbook: Memories of the Homes of Grandma Lewis Written for Her Grandchildren." Manuscript. Philadelphia, 1896. Excerpts on Library Company of Philadelphia website: "Ice Skating in 19th Century America: A Pictorial View." http://www.librarycompany.org/skating/iceskating.htm.

Lewis, John Frederick. *The Redemption of the Lower Schuylkill: The River As It Was, the River As It Is, the River As It Should Be.* Philadelphia: City Parks Association, 1924.

Magee's Centennial Guide of Philadelphia, 1815. Reprint, Philadelphia: Nathan Cohen Books, 1975.

"Meriwether Lewis." *Lifelong Learning Online: The Lewis & Clark Rediscovery Project.* http://www.13lewisandclark.com/ShowOneObject.asp?SiteID=74&ObjectID=690.

Mowad, Michelle. "History of the Waterway." *Times Herald,* October 30, 2002. http://www.timesherald.com/site/news.cfm?newsid=6230819&BRD=1672&PAG=461&dept_id=33380&rfi=8.

Nolan, J. Bennett. *The Schuylkill.* New Brunswick: Rutgers University Press, 1951.

Pennell, Elizabeth Robins. *Our Philadelphia.* Philadelphia: Lippincott, 1914.

Pennsylvania Horticultural Society. *From Seed to Flower: Philadelphia 1681–1876.* Philadelphia: Pennsylvania Horticultural Society, 1976.

Philadelphia Skating Club and Humane Society. "Club History." http://www.pschs.org /club_history.htm.

Phillyhistory.org. Photograph archive and weblog. http://www.phillyhistory.org/.

Places in Time website. "Places in Time: Historical Documentation of Place in Greater Philadelphia." http://www.brynmawr.edu/iconog/frdr.html.

Rinker, Harry L. *The Schuylkill Navigation: A Photographic History.* Berkeley Heights, NJ: Canal Captain's Press, 1991.

Roberts, Christopher. "The Waterworks: A Place Wondrous to Behold." *Delaware River Basin Education Web.* http://www.state.nj.us/drbc/edweb/waterworks.htm.

Rosenthal, Leon S. *A History of Philadelphia's University City.* Philadelphia: West Philadelphia Corp., 1963.

Sachdev, Glen. "River Phoenix." *Philadelphia Weekly,* June 18, 2003. http://www. philadelphiaweekly.com/view.php?id=5757.

Scharf, J. Thomas, and Westcott, Thompson. *History of Philadelphia.* Philadelphia: L. H. Everts, 1884.

Schuylkill River Greenway Association. "Schuylkill River Trail System." http://www.schuylkillriver.org.

———. "Schuylkill River Water Trail." http://www.schuylkillriver.org.

"Schuylkill Watershed Conservation Plan." http://www.schuylkillplan.org/index.html.

Stevick, Philip. *Imagining Philadelphia: Travelers' Views of the City from 1800 to the Present.* Philadelphia: University of Pennsylvania Press, 1996.

Strahan, Edward, ed. *A Century After: Picturesque Glimpses of Philadelphia and Pennsylvania.* Philadelphia: Allen, Lane, Scott and J. W. Lauderbach, 1875.

Strangers Guide in Philadelphia to All Public Buildings, Places of Amusement, Commercial, Benevolent, and Religious Institutions, and Churches, Principal Hotels etc., etc. Philadelphia: Lindsay & Blakiston, 1860.

Sweeney, Joe. "The History of the Penn Athletic Club Rowing Association: A Saga of a Philadelphia Rowing Club." http://www.boathouserow.org/pac/pachist1.html.

"Tidal Schuylkill River Master Plan: Creating a New Vision." Prepared for the Schuylkill River Development Corporation. EDAW, March 2003.

U.S. Army Corps of Engineers. "Description of Study Area and Its Resources." In *South River Review Study: Pennsylvania Main Report, 1981.* Harrisburg: Commonwealth of Pennsylvania, 1981.

"Vesper Boat Club: All Together." http://www.vesperboatclub.org/
AboutVesper.html#Anchor-Monica-49575.

Wallace, Anthony F. C. *King of the Delawares: Teedyuscung 1700–63*. Philadelphia:
University of Pennsylvania Press, 1949.

Wallace, A. W. Paul. *Indians in Pennsylvania*. Harrisburg: Pennsylvania Historical and
Museum Commission, 1999.

Watson, John Fanning. *Watson's Annals of Philadelphia and Pennsylvania:
A Collection of Memoirs, Anecdotes, and Incidents of the City and Its Inhabitants
and of the Earliest Settlements of the Inland Part of Pennsylvania from the Days
of the Founders*. 1857; http://www.rootsweb.com/~usgenweb/pa
/philadelphia/watsontoc.htm.

Webster, Richard. *Philadelphia Preserved: Catalog of the Historic American Buildings
Survey*. Philadelphia: Temple University Press, 1976.

Weigley, Russell F., ed. *Philadelphia: A 300 Year History*. New York: W.W. Norton, 1982.

"Welcome to the Schuylkill River." http://www.web-savvy.com/river/schuylkill/.

Wister, Jones. *Reminiscences*. Philadelphia: printed for private circulation by J. B.
Lippincott, 1920. Excerpts at http://www.phillyh2o.org/backpages/JonesWister.htm.

Wolf, Edwin, 2nd. *Philadelphia: Portrait of an American City*. Philadelphia: Camino
Books, 1990.

Wright, James. "Leaving the Temple in Nîmes." In *Above the River: The Complete Poems*.
New York: Farrar, Straus and Giroux, 1990.

"Yellow Fever Attacks Philadelphia, 1793." http://www.eyewitnesstohistory.com/
pfyellowfever.htm.

Beth Kephart, the award-winning author of eighteen books, teaches creative nonfiction at the University of Pennsylvania, writes about memory and place for the *Philadelphia Inquirer*, and serves as the strategic writing partner in the boutique communications firm Fusion. Her acclaimed Philadelphia stories—*Flow: The Life and Times of Philadelphia's Schuylkill River*; *Dangerous Neighbors*, a Centennial-era novel; and *Dr. Radway's Sarsaparilla Resolvent*, a *Kirkus* Best Book of the Year—arose from her passion for her city.